Grammar Dimensions

Book Two, Second Edition
Instructor's Manual

Form, Meaning, and Use

Heidi Riggenbach
University of Washington

Virginia Samuda
Sonoma State University

Heinle & Heinle Publishers
An International Thomson Publishing Company

I T P

Pacific Grove • Albany • Bonn • Boston • Cincinnati • Detroit • London
Madrid • Melbourne • Mexico City • New York • Paris
San Francisco • Tokyo • Toronto • Washington

CONTENTS

INTRODUCTION

FROM THE SERIES DIRECTOR

ABOUT THE SERIES

Grammar Dimensions, Second Edition, is a comprehensive and dynamic, four-level series designed to introduce English-as-a-second or foreign language students to the form, meaning, and use of English grammatical structures with a communicative orientation. The series has been designed to meet the needs of students from the beginning to advanced levels and includes the following:

- *Grammar Dimensions, Book 1* beginning/high beginning
- *Grammar Dimensions, Book 2* intermediate
- *Grammar Dimensions, Book 3* high intermediate
- *Grammar Dimensions, Book 4* advanced

The textbooks are supplemented by workbooks, cassettes, instructor's manuals with tests, and a CD-ROM entitled *Grammar 3D*.

THE STORY OF GRAMMAR DIMENSIONS

Everywhere I went teachers would ask me, "What is the role of grammar in a communicative approach?" These teachers recognized the importance of teaching grammar, but they associated grammar with form and communication with meaning, and thus could not see how the two easily fit together.

Grammar Dimensions was created to help teachers and students appreciate the fact that grammar is not just about form. While grammar does indeed involve form, in order to communicate, language users also need to know what the forms mean and when to use them appropriately. In fact, it is sometimes learning the meaning or appropriate use of a particular grammar structure that represents the greatest long-term learning challenge for students, not learning to form it. For instance, learning when it is appropriate to use the present perfect tense instead of the past tense, or being able to use two-word or phrasal verbs meaningfully represent formidable learning challenges for ESL students.

The three dimensions of form, meaning and use can be depicted in a pie chart with their interrelationship illustrated by the three arrows:

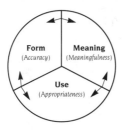

Helping students learn to use grammatical structures accurately, meaningfully, and appropriately is the fundamental goal of *Grammar Dimensions*. It is a goal consistent with the goal of helping students to communicate meaningfully in English, and one that recognizes the undeniable interdependence of grammar and communication.

ABOUT THE BOOKS

The books have been designed to allow teachers to tailor their syllabi for different groups of students. Some teachers have told us that they prefer to teach the units in a different order from that of the book. Teachers should feel free to do so or only to teach part of one unit and then return to do another part at a later time. Since the acquisition process is not a linear one (students do not completely master one structure before moving on to tackle another), teachers can construct syllabi which permit a recycling of material that causes their students difficulty. Of course, some teachers and students would rather use the book more conventionally, as well, by working their way through the units chronologically.

To allow for this possibility, some thought has been given to the sequencing of units within a book. The units have been ordered following different principles depending upon the level of the book. In Book 1, where students are introduced (or reintroduced in the case of false beginners) to basic sentence and subsentence grammatical structures and grammatical forms associated with semantic notions such as time and place, the units have been sequenced following conventional linguistic grading, building from one structure to the next. In Book 2, basic sentence and subsentence grammatical structures are dealt with once again. In addition, Book 2 introduces language forms that support certain social functions such as making requests and seeking permission. At this level, units that share certain features have been clustered together. No more than three or four units are clustered at one time, however, in order to provide for some variety of focus. Although the four skills are dealt with in all of the books, the listening and speaking skills are especially prominent in Books 1 and 2.

Clustering 2–3 units that address related topics has been done for levels three and four as well. Book 3 deals with grammatical structures that ESL/EFL students often find challenging, such as the use of infinitives and gerunds. It also employs a discourse orientation when dealing with structures such as verb tenses and articles. Students learn how to use grammar structures accurately within contexts above the level of the single sentence. Book 4 deals with grammatical forms that are especially needed for academic and technical writing. It reveals to students the subtleties of certain grammatical structures and how they contribute to cohesion in discourse. Both books highlight the reading and writing skills and target structures for which students at these levels can benefit from special guidance in order to avoid their learning plateauing and their errors fossilizing.

NEW FEATURES IN THE SECOND EDITION

Teachers who have taught with *Grammar Dimensions* will note that the basic philosophy and approach to teaching grammar have not changed from the first edition. We believe they are still sound linguistically and pedagogically, and users of the first edition have confirmed this. However, our series users have also requested several new features, and modifications of others, and we have carefully woven these into this second edition:

1. One new feature that series users will notice is the incorporation of listening. Each unit has at least one activity in which students are asked to listen to a taped segment and respond in some way that involves the target structures.
2. A second new feature is the inclusion of a quiz after every unit to help teachers assess what students have learned from the unit. These 10- or 15-minute quizzes are available for duplication from the Instructor's Manuals.
3. Another change we have implemented is to streamline the grammar explanations and make them more user-friendly. You will notice that grammar terms are consistently labeled in the most straightforward and common manner. Also, note that in each focus box examples are consistently outlined on the left and explanations on the right to enhance clarity.
4. In response to user feedback, we have limited the texts to 25 units each. As was mentioned above, the material is meant to be used selectively, not comprehensively; still, some users preferred that the books have fewer units to begin with, and we agree that a reduced scope of grammatical topics in each book will help both teachers and students focus more successfully on their greatest learning challenges.
5. To honor the multiplicity of learning styles in the classroom and to capitalize on the dynamism of emerging technologies, we have developed a CD-ROM component called *Grammar 3D* to complement the *Grammar Dimensions* print materials. A wealth of exciting exercises and activities in *Grammar 3D* review and expand upon the lessons presented in the textbooks.

In all these ways, it is our hope that this series will provide teachers with the means to create, along with their students, learning opportunities that are tailored to students' needs, are enjoyable, and will maximize everyone's learning.

SERIES COMPONENTS

Each level of *Grammar Dimensions*, 2e, consists of the following components:

- **Student Book.**
- **Audio Cassette.** The audio cassettes contains the listenings from the communicative activities (purple pages) in the student text. An icon ✎ indicates which activities use the audio cassette.
- **Workbook.** The workbook provides additional exercises for each grammar point presented in the student text. Many of the workbook exercises are specially designed to help students prepare for the TOEFL® (Test of English as a Foreign Language).
- **Teacher's Manual.**
- **CD-ROM (*Grammar 3D*).** *Grammar 3D* is a CD-ROM program that provides comprehensive instruction and practice in 34 of the key grammar structures found in the text series.

Grammar 3D is appropriate for high-beginning to advanced students, and allows students to progress at their own pace. Students can access each grammar category at three or four levels of difficulty. They can then move to a lower level if they need basic review, or to a higher level for additional challenge.

An instructional "help page" allows students to access grammar explanations before they begin an exercise or at any place within an exercise. Instruction is also provided through feedback that helps students understand their errors and guides them toward correct answers.

An icon appears in the student text next to the focus boxes that are supported by exercises in *Grammar 3D*.

- ***Grammar Dimensions* Web Site.** Come experience *Grammar Dimensions* on-line, an interactive place for grammar, Internet, and writing activities. http://gd.heinle.com

ABOUT THIS MANUAL

This teacher's manual includes the following:

- General suggestions for teaching with *Grammar Dimensions*.
- Teaching suggestions and answer keys for each unit in the student's book.
- Tests. A 15-minute test is included for each unit. You can administer after each unit or combine with others to create longer tests. Teachers are welcome to photocopy the tests for student use.
- Answer key for tests.
- Answer key for workbooks.
- Tapescripts for listenings that appear in the communicative activities section (purple pages) of each unit of the Student's Book.

GENERAL TEACHING SUGGESTIONS

OPENING TASK

Our time with our students is very precious. We must seek ways to put it to their best advantage. In order to do this, you need to learn what your students know and don't know how to do. This will allow you to target what you teach to what your students don't know, and therefore, need to learn. This is the major purpose of the opening task. You should be able to obtain invaluable information about your students' learning needs from "reading" (closely observing) your students as they go about doing the task. Each task has been constructed so that students will need to use the target structures in order to complete it. As the students are focused on completing the task, you are freed to learn as much as you can about your students' learning needs. It will probably be best if, after you have introduced the task (making sure students know what they are being asked to do), you have the students carry out as much of the task as they can by themselves. This will allow you to more closely observe your students' performance.

One way of doing this is to circulate in the classroom and "eavesdrop" on small group discussions. Take mental or written notes on your observations. Pay particular attention to how accurate, meaningful, and appropriate your students' use of the target structures is. Hold up the form, meaning, and use pie chart in your mind and see if you can determine where they have been successful and where they need help. At this point, it is probably better if you refrain from any error correction. The tasks are supposed to encourage students to work meaningfully without concern that they will be interrupted, evaluated, or corrected. The only exception might be the need to remind students to work in English if they are using another language.

Sometimes the tasks involve individual written performances. When this is the case, study carefully what your students write. They, too, can provide valuable clues about what students can and cannot do. In many cases, students will want to hear each other's solutions to the questions or problems posed in the task. This provides yet another excellent opportunity for you to listen to your students and learn what has been easy for them and what has been difficult.

Of course, as with anything, different difficulties are likely to arise for different students. To cope with differing learning needs, you may consider grouping students with similar problems in class and giving each group different exercises to work through and/or different homework assignments. Another possibility is to group students in such a way that students who already know certain aspects of the target structure are grouped with other students who don't. In this way, students can learn from one another as they work through the focus boxes and exercises. If you do group students in this manner, however, it is important that each student be given a role in the group, so that students who are struggling with the content can still be contributing members of the group. For example, give these students the assignment of recording the group's answers or of reporting them to another group or to the whole class.

Obviously, if students demonstrate no ability to use the target structures required in completing the task, you will need to work systematically through the unit. It may be the case, though, that you will discover that students do not need to attend to all the focus boxes or do all the exercises; this makes your teaching more efficient.

Also, don't hesitate to alter tasks to fit your timetable. For example, have your students do only part of the task, or have them do one of the communicative activities at the end of the unit if you feel that the opening task would not work as well. Other teachers have found it helpful to have students do the task twice—first for diagnostic purposes and second after students have worked through a unit in order to determine how much they have progressed.

All in all, what we are trying to achieve is an optimal use of the time we have available by identifying teachable moments when the students need to and are ready to learn.

FOCUS BOXES

The focus boxes feature the form, meaning, and use facts concerning the target structure that are appropriate for students at a given level of instruction. By treating one aspect of the structure at a time, followed by exercises providing practice, the focus boxes allow students to develop step-by-step a better understanding of, and an ability to use, the structure accurately, meaningfully, and appropriately.

Use student performance on the opening task as a bridge to the focus boxes. One way to do this is to write on the blackboard students' responses to the task, eliciting or supplying the target structures as they are needed. By going back and pointing out the target structures and asking questions about their form, meaning, or use, you may be able to induce the rules in the focus boxes (not all at once, of course). At this point, you may want students to consult the relevant focus box in order to confirm the generalizations they have just made. On the other hand, if the students have arrived at the generalizations you feel they need to know, you may simply want to call their attention to the appropriate focus boxes for them to refer to for homework or when needed.

If you prefer a more deductive approach, you could go right to the first or appropriate focus box after the students have completed the task. You could present it orally to students or read it while they listen or read along silently with you. Alternatively, you could have the students read the focus boxes for homework or silently in class. You could help them when they do not understand something. You could check their understanding by asking students to come up with additional examples to supplement the ones in the focus box or asking them to compare how the material in this box differs from one earlier in the unit or from those in a related unit that they have completed.

A variation on this is to ask students individually or in pairs to present the information in a focus box to another pair of students, or even to the whole class, adding a few new examples of their own. Teaching something to others is a great way to learn!

Another possible way of teaching the focus boxes is not to present them at all, but rather to assign students the exercises that go along with them. The focus boxes can be used for reference purposes as the students work their way through the exercises. In this way, the material becomes more meaningful to students because they will need to access and understand it in order to do something with it.

EXERCISES

At least one exercise follows each focus box. There is a wide variety of exercises in *Grammar Dimensions*. There are both comprehension and production exercises. Comprehension exercises work on students' awareness and understanding. Production exercises develop students' skill in using the structures.

There are exercises that are consistent with the theme of the task and ones that introduce students to new themes and vocabulary in order to provide variety and to foster students' ability to transfer their learning to new contexts. There are personalized exercises, in which students use their own background knowledge or opinions to answer questions, and ones where students use the information that is supplied in order to complete the exercise.

Then, too, although general directions are provided for each exercise, there is a great deal of flexibility in how the exercises can be handled. Some exercises, such as information gaps, call for pair work. Others are amenable to many different student configurations—individual, pair, small group, whole class—so you will need to decide what works best for a particular exercise and particular group of students. For instance, some students prefer to work individually at first and then get

together with others to go over their answers. The variety of possible student configurations that the exercises permit allows you to cater to students' differing learning styles.

Sometimes you can choose freely whether to have students do an exercise orally or in writing. At other times, an exercise will work better in one modality than another because of the modality in which the structure normally occurs. Some exercises may be done in class, others for homework, and still others skipped all together. Don't forget to consult the workbook for additional exercises.

There are also many options for checking the students' exercise answers. For example:

1. You can circulate while students are doing an exercise in class and spot-check.
2. You can go over the exercise as a whole class afterwards and call on each student to supply an answer.
3. Exercises can be done individually and then pairs of students can get together to check their answers with each other. Where a difference of opinion occurs, you (or another pair of students) can act as referee.
4. Different students, pairs, or groups of students can be assigned different parts of an exercise. For example, the first group does 1-5; the second group does 6-10, etc. The groups post their answers on newsprint or butcher block paper and everyone circulates at the end noting the answers and asking questions.
5. A variation of number 4 above is to have one student from each group come together to present the exercise answers that his or her group came up with to the other students.
6. You can prepare a handout with the answers and have each student correct his or her answers individually.
7. You can collect the written work and make a list of common errors. You can put the errors on an overhead transparency and show it to the students during the next class and have them correct the errors together.

There are both closed and open-ended answers to questions. With closed questions, there is a single right answer. This is the most common type of question in Book 1 and 2. In Books 3 and 4, while closed questions still prevail, sometimes open-ended questions, for which there are no definitive answers, are used. Nuances of the language and contextual differences are such that it is sometimes difficult to say definitively what the single best answer is. The point is that students should understand that they have choices, but they also need to understand the consequences of their choices, i.e., they should be able to explain why they have chosen a particular answer. In many of these cases a "most likely" interpretation (based on English native-speaker responses) has been indicated in the answer key that follows, but no feasible opinion offered by your students should be discounted. Giving students an opportunity to defend their answers encourages them to form their own hypotheses about the appropriate use of certain grammar structures and to test these hypotheses through continued observation and analysis.

ACTIVITIES

In the activities section of each unit (the purple pages), students can apply the language discussed in the unit to wider contexts and integrate it with the language they already know. Many activities give students more control over what they want to say or write than the exercises and offer them more opportunities to express their own points of view across a range of topics. Most of the activities are quite open-ended in that they lend themselves to being done with structures covered in the unit, but they do not absolutely require their use.

The activities section is also designed to give instructors a variety of options. Since time is limited, you probably will not be able to have students do all the activities. You might choose two to do or ask your students to choose ones that they would prefer. Perhaps different groups of students could do different activities and then report on their experience to the whole class. Like the exercises, the activities can be adapted for use with different group configurations and different modalities.

If you are teaching in a program that is skill-based, you might want to collaborate with your colleagues and distribute the activities among yourselves. For example, the writing teacher could assign the activities that involve a written report, the teacher of listening could work on the listening activities during his or her class periods, or the teacher of speaking could work with students on activities where students are supposed to make an oral presentation.

Although the activities are meant to be culminating, it is also possible to intersperse them among the exercises. Sometimes an activity provides a particularly useful follow-up to an exercise. And we have already mentioned that certain activities might work well in place of the recommended opening task. Also, it may be useful to go back to a previous unit and do an activity for review purposes. This is especially useful at the beginning of a new, but related, unit.

Activities are an integral part of each unit because they not only provide students with opportunities to stretch their language use, but, as with the opening task, they also provide you with the opportunity to observe your students' language use in action. In this way, activities can be informal holistic assessment measures encouraging students to show you how well they can use the target structures communicatively. Any persistent problems that still exist at this point can be noted for follow-up at a later time when students are more ready to deal with them.

As you can see, *Grammar Dimensions* is meant to provide you with a great deal of flexibility so that you can provide quality instruction appropriate for your class.

We encourage you to experiment with different aspects of the material in order to best meet the needs of your unique group of students.

TEACHING A SAMPLE UNIT

UNIT 2 PRESENT PROGRESSIVE AND SIMPLE PRESENT

It is necessary to set this task up quite carefully. First of all, explain that the small pictures are all part of ONE larger picture. Emphasize that they are not a set of unrelated pictures, but all connect up to form a whole—i.e. the same picture. The task is to guess a) where this probably is and b) what is probably happening. If they want, students can draw in the missing parts of the picture.

Students should work in pairs or groups.

To set things in motion, you could ask (or write on the board): Where do you think this is? A hospital? A park? A classroom? A store? A restaurant? Somewhere else? And encourage students to include a guess about the location as they try to figure out what's going on in the whole picture. The drawing is deliberately ambiguous and generally sparks a lot of discussion. If you circulate while the students are working, you can get an idea of their current use (or non- use) of the present progressive. Accuracy of course is not important at this stage.

Since in our experience students are pretty curious about what other classmates think is happening, you could bring the class together and get different pairs/groups to talk about what they think is going on and why. If there are several different versions, you could have students vote on which version that they think is most likely.

There are many ways to make a bridge between this task and the first focus box, depending on your preference. If some students come up with present progressive sentences as they explain their pictures, you could put them up on the board. Alternatively, if students do not give accurate versions of the present progressive, you could reframe their examples so that they include present progressive and write them on the board. Later, once all the solutions have been discussed, you could underline the present progressive verbs and invite generalizations about why this form has been used. Students thus induce rules from their own examples. Exercises 1 and 2 bring students back to the Task and focus on accuracy. Students can check their guesses against the complete picture on page AK-2 after Exercise 1.

EXERCISE 1:

Answers will vary depending on students' perceptions.

EXERCISE 2:

Answers will vary.

EXERCISE 3:

1. b 2. a 3. b 4. b 5. a 6. a

EXERCISE 4:

1. B: am washing   2. A: are you doing B: am/'m taking; am/'m learning   3. A: are/'re studying; always have   4. A; are...doing; hardly ever write   5. B: is/'s raining A: does it always rain; never rains   6. A: is...wearing B: generally goes   7. A: gets up; plays; does; makes; do not/don't get; like; am/'m waking B: is/'s she doing A: is/'s sleeping; goes

EXERCISE 5:

Answers are also on page AK-3.

1.   I love you   2. I see you   3. I hate you
4. I hear you   5. He knows you   6. Are you 21?
7. I see you are too wise for me.
8. I think you are great.

Emotions and feelings: love, hate   *Senses and perceptions:* see, hear   *Cognition:* know, think   *Verb that does not fit:* be

In common: All these verbs are not *usually* used in the progressive when you want to express a state or situation we do not expect to change.

EXERCISE 6:

(1) are discovering   (2) is becoming   (3) is growing
(4) produces   (5) sell   (6) manages   (7) are
(8) own   (9) ride   (10) are riding   (11) believe
(12) provide   (13) sells   (14) is selling   (15) comes
(16) buys   (17) does not/doesn't own   (18) likes
(19) hates   (20) is not/isn't   (21) knows   (22) think
(23) are

Note: Board game format; not every number requires an answer.

2. is/'s sitting/sits   **3.** does not/doesn't know   **5.** are spending   **6.** do you think; is/'s thinking   **7.** smell   **9.** have   **10.** are/'re studying   **11.** Do you like; love   **12.** is/'s having; has   **13.** think; is/'s taking   **14.** Do you always take; walk   **15.** Do you like; hate   **16.** do not/don't see   **18.** does she own   **19.** weighs   **20.** am/'m having   **21.** is/'s taking; takes   **22.** are having   **24.** is/'s writing; writes   **25.** love   **26.** is/'s tasting; tastes   **28.** is/'s bleeding

Activity 1:

See tapescript for answers.

TEACHING SUGGESTIONS AND ANSWER KEYS

Unit 1

Simple Present

Habits, Routines, and Facts

OPENING TASK

The purpose of this task is not only to introduce the language focused on in this unit, but also to help you get a feel for the ideas about grammar learning that your students bring with them to the classroom. The task may also enable you to raise awareness of the fact that there are many ways to approach the learning and teaching of grammar, some of which may be new to your students. You may find it helpful to share something of your own philosophy of grammar teaching and learning.

To set up the task, you could model what has to be done by reading each statement aloud and checking that the students understand, glossing vocabulary as necessary. Emphasize that there are no wrong or right answers. You could also do the questionnaire, based on your own experiences as a language learner.

Step 1: Students work individually and complete the questionnaire. It isn't necessary to wait until everyone has finished, as students are bound to finish at different times. Those who finish early can pair up with each other and proceed to Step 2. If students do finish at about the same time, you might want to group them according to different educational and cultural backgrounds.

Step 2: Students work in pairs or groups of three to compare their answers and to complete the chart. Encourage them to add anything that they do that isn't on the chart.

Step 3: Bring the class together to share and compare their findings. In a large class, it may be time-consuming and tedious for all pairs to report back. If you circulate and monitor during Step 2, you can call on pairs who have something interesting/different/provocative to contribute. Alternatively, you could kick off Step 3 by sharing your responses to the questionnaire, expanding and elaborating on them with examples from your own experiences as a language learner, inviting responses from the students in the light of their experiences and how they have completed the questionnaire.

As a wrap-up to the task, you could conduct an informal poll of learning preferences based on the question: How many people in this room think of grammar rules when

they speak? Answers can be recorded on the board or on poster paper. (NOTE: You should be ready to deal with the fact that answers may vary according to the context in which English is used; for example, in #10, the response may depend on what type of student is speaking and to whom.) You could then draw on this information to weave in the information in Focus 1.

It is not necessary to deal with accuracy during Steps 1 - 3. The purpose of the task is to create a context in which the simple present could be used. The students' attention will most likely be focused on meaning, not on form, so this will give you a good opportunity to see to what extent they are able to produce the simple present spontaneously, and enable you to diagnose how much of the unit they will need to work through. Hence, the focus of the task is on meaning, not on form. Exercises 1 and 2 return to the task, giving students the opportunity to review and revise what they wrote in Step 2, and here the focus is on accuracy.

Answers will vary, depending on how students describe themselves in Step 1.

EXERCISE 1

1. study; memorize   2. read; watch; listen   3. use; know   4. observe; notice; say; do   5. (don't) know; (don't) say   6. (don't) worry; help   7. helps 8. uses; (don't) understand; ask   9. don't know; try 10. think; speak

EXERCISE 2

Answers will vary, since it depends on what students wrote in Step 2 of the opening task. It is likely that many of the verbs in Step 1 will be used: study/studies, memorize/memorizes, read/reads, etc. Other possibilities include: like/likes/don't like, prefer/prefers, etc.

EXERCISE 3

It is impossible to predict answers here, as they will obviously depend on students' own experiences. The third part is designed to focus on third person *s*. In the last part, students could write their strategies on butcher paper and display them on the walls or write them in their notebooks. As time passes, they might want to add to their repertoire of strategies.

EXERCISE 4

A. 2 (or 3) B. 1 C. 5 D. 4

EXERCISE 5

Step 1: If there is not enough room in the space provided on the chart, have students copy it into their notebooks. Answers will vary. Depending on the cultural backgrounds of the students, possible answers may include:

Teachers in my country hardly ever talk to students outside class.   Students in my country never ask questions in class.   Teachers in this country usually give homework.   Students in this country sometimes call their teachers by their first names.

EXERCISE 6

Step 1: 1. a flight attendant   2. a businessperson
3. a police officer   4. a bartender   5. a bus driver
6. a student   7. a waitress   8. teachers

Step 2: Answers will vary. For example:
9. Mechanics work with their hands.   10. Secretaries work in offices. They do many different things, but they usually write business correspondence. They sometimes organize meetings and social events. They don't usually work on weekends.   11. A nurse usually works in a hospital, but sometimes she or he works in other places. She or he takes care of people who are sick. She or he works very long hours and usually wears a uniform.
12. An architect designs houses and buildings. He or she draws blueprints and plans for the designs and discusses them with his or her clients. He or she often builds small

models of the building he or she designs and then supervises its construction.

Step 3: # 13 and # 14 depend on what occupations students come up with themselves.

Step 4: Answers will vary.

EXERCISE 7

Some answers will vary.
(2) walk/run/jog   **(3)** do you do   **(4)** take   **(5)** ride
(6) play/watch   **(7)** do you do   **(8)** stay   **(9)** read
(10) watch   **(11)** drive/go   **(12)** swims   **(13)**
swim/go   **(14)** sit/stay/lie   **(15)** meet   **(16)**
don't/do not go/belong   **(17)** dance   **(18)** likes

EXERCISE 8

Step 1: (from left to right)
bat   spider   elephant
bear   scorpion
swan   horse   antelope

Steps 2 and 3:
Horses sleep standing up.   Bats use their ears to "see". Scorpions have twelve eyes.   Elephants sometimes go for four days without water.   Swans stay with the same mates all their lives.   Antelopes run at 70 miles per hour.   Bears sleep during the winter months. Spiders live for about two years.

Step 4: Answers will vary.

Activity 2

The chart in Step 4 is to provide a rough guide only. Students should take notes in their own notebooks.

Activity 3

Check tapescript for answers to fill in chart.

Unit 2

Present Progressive and Simple Present

Actions and States

OPENING TASK

It is necessary to set this task up quite carefully. First of all, explain that the small pictures are all part of ONE larger picture. Emphasize that they are not a set of unrelated pictures, but all connect up to form a whole—i.e. the same picture. The task is to guess a) where this probably is and b) what is probably happening. If they want, students can draw in the missing parts of the picture.

Students should work in pairs or groups.

To set things in motion, you could ask (or write on the board): Where do you think this is? A hospital? A park? A classroom? A store? A restaurant? Somewhere else? Encourage students to include a guess about the location as they try to figure out what's going on in the whole picture. The drawing is deliberately ambiguous and generally sparks a lot of discussion. If you circulate while the students are working, you can get an idea of their current use (or non-use) of the present progressive. Accuracy of course is not important at this stage.

Since in our experience students are pretty curious about what other classmates think is happening, you could bring the class together and get different pairs/groups to talk about what they think is going on and why. If there are several different versions, you could have students vote on which version they think is most likely.

There are many ways to make a bridge between this task and the first focus box, depending on your preference. If some students come up with present progressive sentences as they explain their pictures, you could write the sentences on the board. Alternatively, if students do not give accurate versions of the present progressive, you could reframe their examples so that they include present progressive and write them on the board. Later, once all the solutions have been discussed, you could underline the present progressive verbs and invite generalizations about why this form has been used. Students thus induce rules from their own examples. Exercises 1 and 2 bring students back to the task and focus on accuracy. Students can check their guesses against the complete picture on page AK-2 after Exercise 1.

EXERCISE 1:

Answers will vary depending on students' perception.

EXERCISE 2:

Answers will vary.

EXERCISE 3:

1. b 2. a 3. b 4. b 5. a 6. a

EXERCISE 4:

1. B: am washing   2. A: are you doing B: am/'m taking; am/'m learning   3. A: are/'re studying; always have   4. A: are...doing; hardly ever write   5. B: is/'s raining A: does it always rain; never rains   6. A:

is...wearing B: generally goes   7. A: gets up; plays; does; makes; do not/don't get; like; am/'m waking B: is/'s she doing A: is/'s sleeping; goes

EXERCISE 5:

Answers are also on page AK-3.

1. I love you   2. I see you   3. I hate you   4. I hear you   5. He knows you   6. Are you 21?   7. I see you are too wise for me.   8. I think you are great.

Emotions and feelings: love, hate   *Senses and perceptions:* see, hear   *Cognition:* know, think   *Verb that does not fit:* be

In common: All these verbs are not *usually* used in the progressive when you want to express a state or situation we do not expect to change.

EXERCISE 6:

(1) are discovering   (2) is becoming   (3) is growing   (4) produces   (5) sell   (6) manages   (7) are   (8) own   (9) ride   (10) are riding   (11) believe   (12) provide   (13) sells   (14) is selling   (15) comes   (16) buys   (17) does not/doesn't own   (18) likes   (19) hates   (20) is not/isn't   (21) knows   (22) think   (23) are

EXERCISE 7:

Note: Board game format; not every number requires an answer.

2. is/'s sitting/sits   3. does not/doesn't know   5. are spending   6. do you think; is/'s thinking   7. smell   9. have   10. are/'re studying   11. Do you like; love   12. is/'s having; has   13. think; is/'s taking   14. Do you always take; walk   15. Do you like; hate   16. do not/don't see   18. does she own   19. weighs   20. am/'m having   21. is/'s taking; takes   22. are having   24. is/'s writing; writes   25. love   26. is/'s tasting; tastes   28. is/'s bleeding

Activity 1:
See tapescript for answers.

Unit 3
Talking about the Future
Be Going to and Will

OPENING TASK

If possible, use real fortune cookies to introduce this task. Students should work in pairs or groups.

Step 1: Answers may vary. Intended answers are as follows, but if students can justify other matches that are meaningful and accurate, that's O.K.

SOLUTION: 1. I **2.** F **3.** D **4.** A **5.** E **6.** B **7.** G **8.** C **9.** H **10.** J

You might want to briefly check the answers for Step 1 before Step 2.

Step 2: The purpose is to diagnose students' current productive use of *will* and *going to*. If some pairs/groups finish before others, they can get together with other pairs/groups to share the fortunes that they wrote. Finally, bring the whole class together and have students share the most interesting fortunes. You could write some of these on the board and use them as a bridge to Focus 1.

Exercise 1 returns to the task and gives students the opportunity to revise what they wrote in Step 2 if necessary. The emphasis here is on accuracy.

EXERCISE 1

Answers will vary according to students' work on the opening task.

EXERCISE 2

Answers will vary according to the students' predictions about each other.

EXERCISE 3

2. will **3.** is going to **4.** will/are going to **5.** will **6.** is going to **7.** will **8.** will

EXERCISE 4

Answers will depend on the students' own plans, intentions, or predictions. You might expect answers similar to the following:

1. My partner is going to go to the library after class. *(Plan/intention).* **2.** My partner isn't going to do her homework after this class. *(Plan/intention).* **3.** My partner will have a very successful, career/is going to have a very successful career. *(Prediction)*

EXERCISE 5

1. *going to go* (future plan/intention) **2.** Acceptable (prediction) **3.** Acceptable (prediction) **4.** *is going to* (future plan/intention) **5.** Acceptable (future plan/intention)

EXERCISE 6

1. 're/are going to **2.** I'll **3.** 'm/am going to **4.** 'll/will **5.** 'll/will **6.** will; 'll **7.** are going to **8.** 'll/will **9.** are going to; 'll/will; will

EXERCISE 7

Answers will vary, depending on students' answers.
1. (It looks like) it's going to rain. **2.** (I've decided) I'm going to major in music next year. **3.** I'll bring ... to the potluck (if you think that sounds good). **4.** I'll (be sure to) bring the car back by 9:00. **5.** (It looks like) your books are going to fall out of your backpack.
6. I'm going to go to class today, so I'll take notes for you (if you'd like). **7.** (Watch out! Slow down or) you'll/you're going to hit that little boy! **8.** I'm going to go to "Swan Lake". **9.** I'll do them later. (I've got to go help my friend.) **10.** You will/You're going to ....

Activity 2

If you can obtain empty fortune cookies (available in some grocery stores), students can insert their own fortunes and deliver the fortune cookies to the intended recipient.

Activity 4

Check tapescript for answers.

Activity 5

You could assign different students (or groups of students) to interview specific age groups. For example, several students could be asked to interview elementary school children; others could be assigned to junior high students; others to high school and others to college students. The groups could then see if there are any similarities or differences across the age groups. Alternatively, some students could focus on males and others on females to see if there are any differences or similarities across gender.

Unit 4

Asking Questions

Yes/No, Wh-, Tag Questions

OPENING TASK

Step 1: The cartoon has examples of questions with *How come ...?* We do not expand on questions of this type in the unit. If students ask about this, we suggest pointing out that *How come ...?* questions are similar in meaning to *Why ...?* questions, although the word order differs.

Students should work in pairs or groups for the entire task.

Step 2: Explain that students must use the prompts where indicated, but can use whatever form they like for the last two questions. Exercises 1, 2, and 13 return to the task and focus on accurate use of these question forms.

EXERCISE 1

Answers will vary, but may start with some of these: Can you/have you ever ...?   Would you ...?   Do you know how to ...?   Are you going to ...?

EXERCISE 2

Answers will vary, but may start with some of these: When did you ...?   Where did you ...?   Where do you ...?   What is...?   What is/are the name(s) of ...?   How long have you ...?   Why do you ...?

EXERCISE 3

Answers will vary.
(1) Does she live alone/go to school/have a car/have a job?   (2) Does she smoke/go to school/have a car?   (3) What time does she usually go to sleep?   (4) Do you see her very often?   (5) Where does her family live?   (6) How often does she talk with them?   (7) Is she married/a Lesbian?   (8) Was she ever married?   (9) When did she get divorced?   (10) Do you think she'd be interested in going with me?

EXERCISE 4

For 10, 11, and 16, answers will vary. The others will most likely be:
(1) What is your name?   (2) Where are you from?   (3) How many languages do you speak?   (4) What languages do you speak?   (5) Where were you born?   (6) How many sisters and brothers do you have?   (7) What were your favorite subjects in school?

(8) Why are you taking this class?   (9) What do you like to do in your free time?   (10) What are your favorite ....?   (12) What surprised you when you first came here?   (13) What do you hope to do after you finish taking this class?   (14) What makes you happy?   (15) What makes you angry?

EXERCISE 5

Answers may vary.
1. Why is the closet door closed?   2. What's in the closet?/Where's the broom?   3. Where's the vacuum cleaner?   4. Why do we have to clean the house?   5. Who's coming over for dinner?   6. Where did Pat and Sam meet the Smiths?/How do Pat and Sam know the Smiths?   7. When did they meet them there?/When did that happen?   8. What were the Smiths doing in the garden?/What were the Smiths doing when they met Pat and Sam?   9. How are Pat and Sam getting here?   10. What time is everyone coming over?

EXERCISE 6

Arrows indicate rising or falling intonation.
Answers may vary.
(1) How much did it cost? ↑   (2) What's the movie about? ↓   (3) How long is it? ↓   (4) Where did you see it?/Where was it playing? ↓   (5) How much was the ticket?/How much did it cost? ↓   (6) How much? ↑

EXERCISE 7

Answers may vary.
1. Taiwan   2. Japanese/Thai   3. rice   4. in an apartment/in a house/in a dormitory/on campus/off campus   5. chemistry/botany/etc.   6. take the bus/drive   7. volleyball/etc.

EXERCISE 8

1. G   2. F   3. A   4. C   5. E   6. D   7. B

EXERCISE 9

1. didn't you   2. doesn't he   3. wasn't it   4. don't they   5. is it   6. does he   7. don't they   8. didn't we   9. did you   10. won't she   11. aren't I   12. isn't she   13. will it

EXERCISE 10

4. J   **5.** M   **6.** R   **7.** Q   **8.** N   **9.** E   **10.** B   **11.** I   **12.** L
13. O   **14.** F   **15.** C   **16.** H   **17.** K   **18.** D   **19.** S

EXERCISE 11

(Oral exercise)

EXERCISE 12

Read these questions to the students. They answer *yes* or *no*.
1. He's late, isn't he? **Yes**   **2.** You live in Oregon, don't you? **Yes/No**   **3.** You like me, don't you? **Yes**
4. You're not leaving, are you? **No**   **5.** Her birthday's in June, isn't it? **Yes/No**   **6.** They won't come, will they? **No**   **7.** You eat meat, don't you? **Yes/No**   **8.** You don't understand, do you? **No**   **9.** These are difficult, aren't they? **Yes**

EXERCISE 13

1. (a) No   **2. (a)** Yes **(b)** "No, I don't."   **3. (a)** No
4. (a) No   **5. (a)** Yes **(b)** "Yes, I did."   **6.(a)** No
7. (a) Yes **(b)** "Yes, I'm afraid you are."

EXERCISE 14

Answers will vary.

Activity 1

You have the best ideas about the items that will work with your students. You can use pictures instead of words if you prefer. Some possible items: a television, a comb, an ice cream cone, a cup of coffee, a pair of sneakers, Princess Di, an umbrella, a CD, a hamburger, Arnold Schwarzenegger, a rabbit, a bouquet of roses. The best way to stick things on students' backs is to use Post-Its.

Model how the activity works by having a student stick an item on your back and elicit/model some possible questions. At the end of the activity, if there are still some people left who cannot guess their items, you can let the other students give helpful "hints." For example, "You are very popular in summer." "You come in many different flavors." "You melt if you stay in the sun." Conversely, if some students guess their items very quickly, give them a second item to guess.

Activity 6

The first section of the tapescript has Lisa's answers to questions that are not given. The students listen and write the questions probably asked by an interviewer. The second section includes the full question and answer exchange between Lisa and Gary.

Activity 8

If you prefer, bring in pictures yourself. Large color photographs from magazines are most suitable.

Unit 5

Modals of Probability and Possibility

Could, May, Might, Must

OPENING TASK

It is worth taking some time to set this task up by talking a bit about the kinds of things that people usually carry in their purses, wallets, backpacks, or briefcases. For example, hold up you own purse, briefcase or wallet and invite guesses about what is probably inside. You could also do the same thing with one of the students. The idea to establish is that we can often guess something about the owner of the purse, wallet, etc., from its contents. As students make guesses about what is in your purse/wallet, you can prepare them for the chart by asking: Are you certain? Are you really certain? 100 percent certain? Not very certain? And so on. Don't worry about modal use at this point. The focus here is on preparing students for the chart.

Explain the task situation carefully and go through the chart, checking that students understand what they are to do. If they are 100 percent certain that the mystery person is male, they write "Male" in the 100% column. If they are less than 50 percent certain that he or she is 40 years old, they write "40" in the Less than 50% column, and so on. They do not need to write full sentences, just the relevant piece of information is enough. They will get an opportunity later to convert the information into full sentences, focusing on accuracy (for example, Exercises 2, 4, 9 and 11 and Activities 6 and 7 also revisit the task in a slightly different way).

Students should work in pairs for Step 1 and then move into larger groups for Step 2.

Step 1: Encourage students to examine everything very carefully before completing the chart.

Step 2: Students share and compare their ideas thus far.

There is no wrong or right answer to this task: It all depends on whatever ideas the students come up with. For example, some groups have speculated that this is a business executive who was probably involved in a lot of international trade and is now possibly planning on branching out on his own, setting up an import/export business. Others have argued that it's possible this is a woman.

Bring the whole class together to share their ideas and to establish how certain they are about each one. You could make an overhead transparency of the blank chart or write the headings on the board and fill in the different ideas that students contribute You can then use this as a springboard for the information in Focus 1, by building on students' own ideas to weave in or elicit possible modal uses.

EXERCISE 1

1) could   2) might   3) may   4) must   5) likes
6) could   7) might   8) may   9) must   10) is

EXERCISE 2

Answers are completely dependent on the inferences the students make in the opening task.

EXERCISE 3

For some questions, answers will vary. The choice of modal auxiliary depends on the speaker's certainty. Some possibilities are:
1. may/might/could/must be   2. may/might have a car/walk   3. probably doesn't/must not
4. may/might   5. is   6. must not/probably doesn't anymore   7. must/does, I think

EXERCISE 4

Answers are completely dependent on the inferences the students make in the opening task.

EXERCISE 5

Answers will vary. The choice of modal auxiliary depends on the speaker's certainty.

2. He might be a jockey/a clown/a circus performer. He might have been born that way.   3. He might have a cold/have drunk too much alcohol/be a clown.   4. She could be a construction worker/mechanic/farmer/gardener/housekeeper. She might wash dishes in a busy restaurant. She might have just gotten out of jail.
5. She might be a movie star/fashion model/rock star/politician. She may have won the lottery.   6. He might be a surgeon/pianist/hand model.   7. He might be a gangster/heavy metal rock star/sailor/member of Hell's Angels.

EXERCISE 6

Answers will vary, depending on what students said in Exercise 5.

EXERCISE 7

This story is open to a range of interpretation. The most likely theory:

The victim knew the murderer well (no sign of a forced entry) and may have drunk wine with him or her in her room. The full wine glass suggests that the murderer may have drugged or poisoned the victim by putting something in the wine. The murderer didn't drink from the other glass because he or she knew it was poisoned. The murderer may have long, blond hair and might have worn a shirt or jacket with white buttons. They must have fought or struggled violently at around 11:30 (button, hair, smashed watch). After killing the victim, the murderer might have searched for information or documents in her desk, but he or she must not have found them or might have had to leave before finding what he or she was looking for. The murderer must have left the house by the victim's window. (The doors were locked from the inside.)

Your students' theories about why and how the crime occurred will probably be much more interesting.

EXERCISE 8

Answers depend on students' responses in Exercise 7.

EXERCISE 9

Answers are completely dependent on the inferences the students make in the opening task.

EXERCISE 10

1. might be   2. must   3. might take   4. must have left   5. may have   6. is probably going to (preferable to *could* here because "dark clouds" suggests a greater probability of rain)   7. might have   8. must have been   9. might   10. must have gone   11. must have   12. may have lost   13. could be   14. must be taking   15. may have   16. must be   17. couldn't have   18. might

Answers are dependent on the inferences the students make in the opening task.

Unit 6

Past Progressive and Simple Past with Time Clause

When, While and *As Soon As*

OPENING TASK

To set up this task, you could talk (and ask students) about various well-known detectives in fiction or movies or on TV. Pictures would be a valuable addition. The task illustration is supposed to evoke a 1940s *film noir* atmosphere. Feed in and elicit some key vocabulary as necessary:

murder/murderer/victim/guilty/innocent/-clues/evidence/accuse/murder weapon/suspicious.

Students should work in pairs or groups of three (larger groups are not recommended for this).

You could set up the task situation with the whole class and emphasize that all the clues for solving the murder mystery are in the picture and that the true/false questions will help to find the solution. You might also want to emphasize that these are *probably* true and *probably* false questions.

Students write their opinions about the murder in the box provided. Don't worry about accuracy at this point: Exercises 1, 2, 3, 4, 5, and 6 return to the task in various ways. A number of different theories generally emerge and discussion can be heated.

1. F **2.** F **3.** T **4.** F **5.** T **6.** F **7.** F **8.** F **9.** T **10.** T

Solution: See page AK-3.

EXERCISE 1

Answers are dependent on what students wrote in the opening task.

EXERCISE 2

Answers will vary. Possibilities:
was crossing/walking across the bathroom floor **when** *he slipped on a piece of soap/was getting out of the shower* **when** *he slipped on a piece of soap/died* **when** *he slipped on a piece of soap*

somebody killed him **while** *he was brushing his teeth*

EXERCISES 3, 4, AND 5

NOTE: Students are only expected to match the sentence parts in this exercise. However, in Exercise 5, students will be expected to write the sentence in full and add punctuation (as shown here). The underlined parts of each sentence are the answers to Exercise 4; the underlined and bold-face commas are the answers to Exercise 5.

1. Mrs. Meyer called the police <u>as soon as her husband died.</u>   **2.** <u>While she was waiting for the police to arrive**,**</u> she placed a bar of soap on the bathroom floor.   **3.** <u>As soon as Phil Fork heard about the murder**,**</u> he rushed to the Meyers' house.   **4.** When Fork asked to see the body, <u>Mrs. Meyer took him to the scene of the crime.</u>
5. <u>While Fork was searching the bathroom for clues**,**</u> he became suspicious of Mrs. Meyer's story.   **6.** He saw that Mr. Meyer died <u>while he was brushing his teeth.</u>
7. <u>When Fork accused Mrs. Meyer of murder**,**</u> she said that she was innocent.   **8.** A crowd of news reporters tried to interview Mrs. Meyer <u>while the police were taking her to jail.</u>

EXERCISE 6

1. b **2.** a **3.** b **4.** a **5.** b **6.** b **7.** a

EXERCISE 7

The goal of the first part of the exercise is to activate background knowledge and to prepare for the exercise. It offers an opportunity for genuine information exchange as students brainstorm ideas. This exchange works best in groups. Before starting the exercise itself, have the groups share the information they already know about John Lennon. Whether they use past progressive or not doesn't matter at this point. Possible answers include (depending on knowledge and level of interest):

He was born in Liverpool, England.   He was a member of the Beatles.   His second wife was Japanese.

He was killed by one of his fans in New York City. He believed in peace and love and was against war. His son Julian is a singer.

In the chart, the wavy line indicates the action in progress and the "X" indicates a completed action.. The exercise requires the students to combine the two pieces of information, using *when* or *while* as indicated.

(2) He met Paul McCartney ... he was attending high school. **(3)** ... he was studying at art school, he formed the Beatles. **(4)** He was performing in clubs in Liverpool ... he signed his first recording contract. **(5)** He fell in love with Yoko Ono ... he was living in London. **(6)** ... was working for peace and writing new songs ... he died. **(7)** ... one of his fans shot him ... he was leaving his apartment.

EXERCISE 8

You might want to point out to students that the sentences build on each other to make a "story."
1. went **2.** was waiting; came **3.** got; worked/were working **4.** saw; were **5.** realized **6.** were waiting; talked and laughed **7.** was; did not want **8.** left; made **9.** was leaving; said

Activity 1

There are many ways to complete the written part of this activity. One is to have the students write Nan Silveira's life story together after they have completed the information gap activity. Give each pair (or group, if you prefer) a large sheet of newsprint or butcher paper and felt-tip pens. Each pair can affix their paper to the wall in order to write their story. This means students can circulate freely to consult with each other and can compare their versions of Nan's story with their classmates'. It is also easy for you to circulate and advise as necessary as you watch the stories unfold. Alternatively, you can assign the written part of the activity as homework.

Answers will vary.
Nan Silveira graduated from Arizona State University in 1975. In 1976, she sailed across the Pacific Ocean alone and after that she traveled for several years in Asia and India. While she was traveling, she fell in love with a

French doctor and started studying French. In 1979, she went to France and continued her study of French. In 1981, she got a job in Paris, but while she was working there, she broke up with her boyfriend. After that she returned to the U.S. and entered the University of Oregon. She got married in 1985 while she was studying journalism, and in 1986 she had a baby. While she was looking after her son at home, she began to write a book. She finished the book shortly after her son started school. It became a best-seller and two years later she won the Pulitzer Prize.

Activity 2

The chart is intended as a rough guide only. Ask students to copy it into their notebooks, making sure that they have enough space to record their answers. Emphasize that they need to add a time of their own choosing in the last box. You might need to give a couple of examples: *in December 1996; this time three weeks ago*

To ensure that all students in the class are included in this activity, write the names of all the students on separate slips of paper. Make sure each student's name appears three or four times. Distribute several slips to each student. Students make guesses about the names they receive. If they receive their own names, they exchange the slip for a different one. (Of course they are free to also make guesses about any *other* students in the class.)

Activity 4

Depending on your students and the native speakers they have access to, you could substitute someone different. Some possibilities: Kurt Cobain, Jerry Garcia, Martin Luther King, Jr., Malcolm X, Indire Gandhi, Anwar Sadat. Alternatively, you could substitute an important event, for example, the first moon landing, the eruption of Mt. St. Helens (Washington state), the Loma Prieta earthquake (San Francisco), the Northridge earthquake (Los Angeles), or any local event that is likely to have been shared by native speakers in your region.

Activity 5

Speaker 1: England, Standing by fish tank.
Speaker 2: L.A., Ironing
Speaker 3: Phoenix, AZ, Working at ad agency

Unit 7

Similarities and Differences

Comparatives, Superlatives, *As ... As, Not As .... As*

OPENING TASK

Many students enjoy the challenge of this kind of logical problem-solving task. If you can, bring in some of your own group photographs—family, friends, a class group, former students, or whatever—and talk a bit about the people in the photo. This makes a natural bridge to the illustration, where you can point out that, as in the real photos, all the figures in this picture are facing forward, looking out at you. Draw attention to "The Left" and "The Right."

We recommend pairs or at most groups of three for this task.

If one group finishes before the rests, disperse the group members among the remaining groups to advise or help. The group that finishes first can also explain the correct solution to the rest of the class.

SOLUTION: See page AK-4.

EXERCISE 1

1. <u>than</u> F   2. tall<u>er</u> T   3. young<u>er than</u> F
4. tall<u>er than</u> F   5. <u>than</u> F   6. <u>the</u> old<u>est</u> T
7. older than F   8. young<u>est</u>; <u>the</u> old<u>est</u> T   9. <u>the</u> tall<u>est</u>; <u>the</u> old<u>est</u> T   10. <u>The</u> old<u>est</u>; short<u>er than the</u> young<u>est</u> F

EXERCISE 2

Answers will vary.

EXERCISE 3

2. Susan is not as tall as Frank./Susan is shorter than Frank./Frank is taller than Susan.   3. Linda is almost/nearly/not quite/practically as tall as Diana.
4. Carla is not as tall as Linda./Linda is taller than Carla./Carla is shorter than Linda.   5. George is (both) older and taller than Susan./Susan is (both) younger and shorter than George.   6. Bob is almost/nearly/not quite/practically as tall as George.
7. Frank is almost/not quite/nearly/practically as old as George.   8. Diana is not as old as Linda./Diana is younger than Linda./Linda is older than Diana.
9. Frank is the tallest.   10. Linda is the oldest.
11. George is exactly as tall as Diana./Diana is exactly as tall as George.

EXERCISE 4

1. luckier   2. (not) as   3. Miriam's   4. than (not <u>that</u>)
5. many (not <u>much</u>)   6. sister's   7. does (not <u>is</u>)
8. than   9. as (not <u>than</u>)

EXERCISE 5

This is a highly productive exercise (and is always very much enjoyed by students) and is well worth the time it takes students to construct the problem. It gives you an excellent opportunity to observe your students' productive use of the language discussed so far. Students should be encouraged to create people of their own for the problem. They should not use information based on the people in the task. In fact, many students choose to write about famous people or their own classmates, which adds to the enjoyment of the exercise. If there is not enough time to solve each other's problems, students could turn the completed problems in to you, and you can try to solve them for "homework."

The chart is a rough guide only. Students should copy the chart into their notebooks, making sure that they have enough space for all the people shown in the picture and enough lines for their clues.

EXERCISE 6

2. Your factories are not (quite) as modern as ours.
3. Your workers are not (quite) as energetic as ours.
4. Your products are not (quite) as well known as ours.   5. Your advertising is not (quite) as effective as ours.   6. Your designs are not (quite) as up-to-date as ours.   7. Your production is not (quite) as fast as ours.   8. The quality of your product line is not (quite) as high as ours.   9. Your factories are not (quite) as clean as ours.   10. Your factories are not (quite) as safe as ours.

EXERCISE 7

Some answers will vary.
2. People in America are not (quite) as friendly or as hospitable as people in my country.   3. Americans are not as polite as people in my country.   4. The cities at home are not as dirty or as dangerous as here./The cities here are not quite as clean or as safe as the cities at home.
5. Americans are not (quite) as hardworking as the people in my country.   6. American food is not as spicy as

the food in my country. **7.** The nightlife at home is not (quite) as boring as the nightlife here./The nightlife here is not as interesting as the nightlife at home. **8.** People don't watch as much TV at home.

Activity 2

Students will probably need to make a bigger chart of their own to record their answers. They could get together in groups to share their responses to this assignment and compile posters that record all the different idioms they find. The poster could then be displayed in the classroom.

Activity 4

Check tapescript for answers.

Activity 5

Some ideas for objects to compare are: an apple and an orange, a car and a bicycle, a VW and a Ferrari, a pizza and a hot dog. However, the best comparison are ones that have some kind of personal relevance to students. For example, two students in the class, two celebrities known to all the class, two places known to all the students, two different classes they are taking, two books/movies they all know, etc.

Unit 8

Measure Words

OPENING TASK

Students should work in groups.

The purpose of the task is to set a context for measure words, not to test a knowledge of cooking. It doesn't matter if students have no idea how to cook, they can guess—and the wilder the guesses, the more fun it can be. If some students do know something about cooking (not necessarily North American cooking, of course), you could arrange groups of students so that each includes someone who has some idea about some kind of cooking.

To set up the task, run through the initial list of ingredients to check that everyone knows what they are. Real examples of some of the items would be valuable (chocolate chips, for example).

> Bring the groups together as a whole class to check each "recipe." Alternatively, you could redivide the class into three groups, with one taking responsibility for salad, another for salad dressing and the third for chocolate chip cookies. Alternatively again, if you are running a bit short of time, you could discuss only one recipe. Students could decide which one. (The salad is simplest; chocolate chip cookies less so.)

> It doesn't matter how the students define the quantities at this point. Exercises 1 - 3 build on and extend the task and focus on accuracy.

> **Step 1:** Salad—lettuce, hard-boiled eggs, cheese, tomatoes. Salad dressing—mustard, salt, vinegar, olive oil, garlic.

> Chocolate Chip Cookies—sugar, salt, chocolate chips, flour, butter, eggs.

EXERCISE 1

Answers depend on students' personal responses to the opening task.

EXERCISE 2

mustard NC   sugar NC   salt NC   lettuce NC
hard-boiled eggs C   cheese NC   vinegar NC
chocolate chips C   tomatoes C   flour NC   olive oil NC   butter NC   eggs C   garlic C

EXERCISE 3

Students should search the picture for clues about the amount of each item.

Jim's Super Salad: (a) head   (b) head   (c) slices
(d) 1/2 pound   (e) cup of

Jim's Super Salad Dressing: (a) tablespoon of   (b) tablespoons of   (c) tablespoon of   (d) teaspoon of
(e) cup of   (f) cup of

Jim's Granny's Old Time Chocolate Chip Cookies:
(a) pound of   (b) cup of   (c) cup of   (d) cups of
(e) teaspoon of   (f) teaspoon of   (g) teaspoon of
(h) cups of

EXERCISE 4

slices (of bacon)   pound (of ground meat)   cloves of (garlic)   cups of (onion)   teaspoon of (salt)
tablespoons (of fresh herbs)   cans of (tomato sauce)

EXERCISE 5

Questions and answers will vary.

EXERCISE 6

Error is in parentheses; correction follows.

Paragraph 1: (several of) *several*   (couple week) *couple of weeks*   (furnitures) *furniture*   (lot of) *lots of/a lot of*

Paragraph 2: (sugars) *sugar*   (milks) *milk*   (mails) *mail*   (many advice) *advice/a lot of advice*   (fifty letter) *fifty letters*   (advices) *advice*   (A few) *A few of*

Paragraph 3: (informations) *information*   (some problem) *some problems*   (couple of problems) *a couple of problems*   (lot of problems) *a lot of problems/lots of problems*   (several time) *several times*

Activity 5
Check tapescripte for answers.

Unit 9

Degree Complements

Too, Enough, and *Very*

OPENING TASK

To set up this task, you could bring in some classified ads from your local newspaper and talk about finding a place to rent, asking students for their own experiences, or you could ask students to talk about where they currently live. Go through the task situation carefully, checking that everyone understands what Maria wants and what she is limited by.

Students should work in groups or pairs.

Step 1: The purpose is to deal with the abbreviations found in classified ads. Check to make sure that everyone understands these. If you prefer, you could do Step 1 as a whole class activity before breaking into groups for the rest.

SOLUTION: apartment, kitchen, bedroom, dining room, small, large, furnished, unfurnished

Step 2: Check that students understand that they have to match the notes with the ad. Possible answers, although they could vary.

1. G   2. A   3. F   4. B   5. E   6. C   7. D

Step 3: Answers will depend on your students. This is an opportunity to see if they are spontaneously producing the target forms. Don't worry about accuracy here: Exercise 1 returns to the task and gives students the chance to review and revise what they wrote.

Step 4: Maria probably chose 5.

EXERCISE 1

Answers depend on students' notes in the opening task.
1. Too small, not enough closets   2. Too large, too expensive

EXERCISE 2

2. You spend too much money.   3. You didn't study enough.   4. You don't get enough exercise.   5. You eat too many snacks.   6. You drink too much coffee.
7. Maybe you shouted too much at the ball game.
8. You didn't add enough salt.   9. Your stereo is too loud.   10. You don't go to the dentist often enough.

EXERCISE 3

Answers will vary.
2. He's not old enough to drive/too young to drive.
3. was too small/wasn't big enough   4. I've had enough/I've eaten too much   5. I'm not old enough to vote/too young to vote   6. are too tight/are too tight for me to wear   7. is too salty   8. is too heavy for me to carry

EXERCISE 4

Expressions of insufficiency underlined; replacement follows.
wasn't enough room too little room for everyone   only had a few chairs had too few chairs   weren't enough glasses were too few glasses   didn't get very much to drink got too little to drink   wasn't enough cake was too little cake for everyone   not enough people wanted to dance too few people wanted to dance   didn't bring enough film brought too little film   only has about ten wedding photographs has too few wedding photographs

NOTE: It's worth pointing out that these changes overload the text with *few* and *much* and that good writing aims at more variety. Students could work together to redress the balance in this text and see how many ways they can vary the style by using other expressions of insufficiency.

This is entirely dependent on students' responses.

EXERCISE 6

2. too hot to 3. too small to carry 4. too 5. very 6. very
7. too busy to call 8. too 9. very 10. too 11. very 12. too

EXERCISE 7

2. not/n't big enough 3. enough 4. too small to eat in
5. enough 6. very 7. too 8. too many 9. not/n't enough
10. too much 11. enough 12. enough 13. too little

14. too many 15. not enough 16. too busy to 17. enough
18. enough

Activity 1

This game could be played in teams of four or five, with a large poster-sized version of the tic-tac-toe game (in the book) affixed to the wall. Assign two teams to each poster. Teams use Post-Its or pieces of paper with some kind of adhesive backing, with X or O marked on each piece of paper. Then follow the directions in the book.

Activities 2 and 3

If there is not enough room in the charts for students to record their answers, have them record answers in their notebooks.

Activity 6

Check tapescript for answers.

Unit 10

Giving Advice and Expressing Opinions

Should, Ought To, Need To, Must, Had Better, Could, and *Might*

OPENING TASK

If you can lay your hands on a real self-help book, it would be a great way to introduce this task. Alternatively, bring in an advertisement promoting a self-help book or video. Once you have established the idea, your students can add any similar ones they know about.

Students should work in pairs or groups of three.

Step 1: You can introduce this as a whole class activity. Draw attention to the books in the illustration and check that the titles are understood. Then give the pairs/groups a few minutes to put their heads together and come up with some ideas. After that, bring the class together to share ideas and predictions. Alternatively you could conduct all of Step 1 as a whole class activity, and move into pairs/groups for Step 2.

Step 2: Pairs/groups read the sample passages at their own pace and match the extract to the title. Alternatively, you can read the extracts aloud, glossing vocabulary where necessary, and then give the pairs/groups time to match the extract and the title on their own.

You can have a whole class check at this point before pairs/groups go to Step 3, or they can go on at their own pace and you can have a whole class check at the end.

A. 3 B. 5 C. 6 D. 1 E. 2 F. 4

Step 3: The purpose is to provide an opportunity to diagnose the students' spontaneous productive use of the target forms, while their attention is focused on meaning rather than form. Students could move into larger groups and compare the advice they came up with. Each group could then choose the piece of advice they think is the most useful, most interesting, or most surprising. Bring the whole class together to compare. Don't worry about accuracy yet: Exercise 1 takes care of this. If some students use the target forms, you might want to write their advice on the board, underline the modal auxiliaries, and invite generalizations before going on to Focus 1. If the target forms don't appear or appear only very haphazardly, you might want to go straight on to Focus 1. Exercise 1 then allows students to revise and rewrite as necessary.

EXERCISE 1

Answers will vary, depending on what students wrote in the opening task.

EXERCISE 2

Answers will vary.

EXERCISE 3

1. must 2. should 3. must 4. mustn't/(shouldn't)
5. mustn't 6. must 7. should 8. should

EXERCISE 4

1. must 2. should/ought to 3. had better
4. should/ought to 5. had better 6. must 7. had better
8. must 9. should 10. had better

EXERCISE 5

1. must not 2. should 3. must not 4. should 5. had better 6.. must 7. had better 8. had better 9. should
10. should

EXERCISE 6

Answers will vary, depending on students' advice and opinions.

EXERCISE 7

This is based on a well-known logic problem with which many students may be familiar. After solving the problem, students often like to share other versions that they know about. The solution is given on page AK-4 in the student book.

EXERCISE 8

Answers will vary, depending on students' advice and opinions.

EXERCISE 9

Answers will vary. If there is not enough room for students to rank the items in their books, they can use their own notebooks.

Activity 7

Speaker agrees with: Smoking should be banned. Should not be able to buy cigarettes in drug stores and supermarkets.

Unit 11

Modals of Necessity and Prohibition

Have To/Have Got To, Do Not Have To, Must/Must Not, Cannot

OPENING TASK

The only thing that you need to do to set this one up is to check that everyone understands "U.S. Immigration and Customs." This is usually not a problem, especially if you present it in the context of the task situation.

Students should work in pairs or groups.

Step 1: You might want to check that everyone understands the vocabulary in the box.

Step 2: Categories 1 and 2 are relatively straightforward because most of the items in this category are bound by U.S. law, so you can expect little disagreement here. Categories 2 and 4 are subjective, however, so expect a fair degree of disagreement. There are no wrong or right answers; it depends on personal opinion. This is deliberate and is designed to focus attention on strong necessity/obligation and prohibition (Categories 1 and 2), and contrast this with weak necessity and absence of necessity.

1. a passport; a tourist visa

2. a gun; fresh fruit (according to California law)

3. Answers will vary depending on individual points of view, but may include: traveler's checks; a credit card; a return airline ticket; photographs of your hometown; reggae tapes and CDs (answers will definitely vary on this one); hiking boots (depending on the type of vacation)

4. Answers will vary depending on individual points of view, but may include: an international driver's license; an umbrella; a business suit; books about Jamaica; a laptop computer; a map of the U.S.; California guide books (can buy them there); a surfboard (can rent one)

If students appear to be having difficulty with this, you could bring them together as a whole group at the end of Step 2 to compare results. You can do this by drawing the chart on the board (or making an overhead transparency) and use student suggestions to fill in the categories.

Step 3: You can use this as a check on students' understanding of Step 2 and add student ideas to those on the blackboard chart or overhead.

Step 4: The point here is that you get a chance to see to what extent students are able to produce these forms when they are concentrating on meaning and not form. Don't worry about accuracy for the moment (see Exercise 1).

You could use students' sentences as a bridge to Focus 1 or you could use the chart you and the students completed in Steps 2 and 3.

EXERCISE 1

Answers will vary, depending on what students wrote in the opening task.

EXERCISE 2

The use of *have to* and *have got to* may vary in students' answers.
1. have to turn right   2. have got to stop.   3. have to yield.   4. has to look out for pedestrians.   5. have got to turn left.

EXERCISE 3

know how to drive   take an eye test   take a written test   pass a driving test   drive on the right

EXERCISE 4

Answers will vary.

EXERCISE 5

1. have got to   2. have to   3. have got to   4. have to; has got to   5. have to

EXERCISE 6

Answers will vary, but will probably include:
You must not/cannot: walk on the grass; pick the flowers; park here; draw or write on the statue; throw bottles in this bin; let your dog walk here/bring dogs here; smoke in the park; ride a bicycle here; climb the trees.

EXERCISE 7

Before starting this exercise, you might want to discuss the possible meaning of the word *token* in this context and the different ways that people can pay for public transportation in the various cities that students know.

In Photograph A, you have to/must buy something to get change, but in Photograph B, you don't have to buy anything to get change.

EXERCISE 8

This depends on students' answers for Exercise 7.

EXERCISE 9

Answers will vary, depending on students' advice and opinions.

EXERCISE 10

Step 1: Corrected answers, based on the reading:
1. T   2. T   3. T   4. T   5. F   6. T   7. F

EXERCISE 11

(1) had to   **(2)** had to   **(3)** had to   **(4)** didn't have to
(5) had to   **(6)** won't have to   **(7)** don't have to
(8) don't have to

EXERCISE 12

In some cases, several answers are possible.
Conversation A: **1.** has to/has got to   **2.** does he have to
3. has to

Conversation B: **4.** must/have got to/have to
5. must/have to/have got to

Conversation C: **6.** have got to/must have to   **7.** have got to/must

Conversation D: **8.** don't have to   **9.** will have to/must
10. had to

Activity 1

This activity works very well in pairs. To set it in motion, you could prepare a series of prohibitions and write each one on a card. (You mustn't feed the ducks/sleep in class/drink the water/bring dogs to this place/carry a gun in this place/write graffiti on the wall/chew gum here, etc.). Each pair takes a card and creates a sign that expresses the meaning. Follow the directions given in the student book.

Activity 2

This chart is a rough guide only. Have students copy this one into their notebooks, leaving plenty of space to record their answers.

Activity 4

Check tapescript for answers.

Unit 12

Expressing Likes and Dislikes

OPENING TASK

Answers are completely dependent on what kinds of food students like and dislike.

EXERCISE 1

Answers are dependent on the statements that students made in the opening task.

EXERCISE 2

Answers will vary, depending on the information students have gathered. The general format should be:

I like ..... and so does my partner.   I don't like ...... and neither does my partner.   I like ..... and my partner does too.   I don't like ..... and my partner doesn't either.

Second paragraph: I don't like ..... and my partner doesn't either.   I don't like ...... and neither does my partner. I like ..... and so does my partner.   I like ..... and my partner does too.

EXERCISE 3

1. d   **2.** j   **3.** I   **4.** g   **5.** f   **6.** a   **7.** b   **8.** c   **9.** k   **10.** h   **11.** e

EXERCISE 4

Top Row (l-r): Panel 1: D/I Panel 2: E/G Panel 3: B
Middle Row (l-r): Panel 4: C/H Panel 5: F Panel 6: D/I
Bottom Row (l-r): Panel 7: G/E Panel 8: H/C Panel 9: A

EXERCISE 5

Answers will vary.
(2) Sort of/Kind of   **(3)** Neither do I/I don't either
(4) I don't either/neither do I   **(5)** Kind of/Sort of
(6) So do I/I do too   **(7)** Sort of/Kind of   **(8)** I do too/So do I   **(9)** So have I/I have too   **(10)** kind of/sort of

EXERCISE 6

1. T   **2.** F   **3.** F   **4.** T   **5.** F   **6.** F   **7.** F

EXERCISE 7

GERUNDS: dancing, eating, walking, camping, hiking , cycling, cooking, jogging

Subjects followed by objects/complements:
1. ∅; walking on the beach   3. Cooking for friends; ∅
5. ∅; dancing   6. ∅; hiking   7. Jogging and cycling; ∅

Activity 3

You could prepare some of the cards yourself to supplement those prepared by the students.

Activity 4

This chart is a rough guide only. Have students copy this one into their notebooks, leaving plenty of space to record their answers.

Activity 5

Check tapescript for answers.

Unit 13

Present Perfect with *Since* and *For*

OPENING TASK

To set up this task, you could talk about going to the doctor. What kinds of information do doctors usually ask about? With a bit of luck, this may elicit many of the headings on the chart.

Students should work in pairs or groups.

PAST: 2. He stopped smoking.

PRESENT: 1. He drinks a glass of wine with dinner. **2.** He weighs 185 lbs.

FROM PAST TO PRESENT: 1. glasses **2.** headaches

Students will probably have difficulty with the last category: PAST TO PRESENT. Use this as a bridge to the information in Focus 1. Exercises 1-4 follow up and build on the task and focus attention on accuracy.

EXERCISE 1

1. c **2.** c **3.** b **4.** b **5.** a **6.** b **7.** c **8.** a **9.** c **10.** a

EXERCISE 2

2. Do you wear glasses? **3.** When did you start wearing them? **4.** Have you worn them for some time? **5.** Do you smoke? **6.** When did you stop? **7.** Have you smoked since then?/since that time? **8.** Have you had these headaches for some time?

EXERCISE 3

Questions and answers will vary, depending on what students choose to talk about.

EXERCISE 4

Since: that time; 1987
For: two months; three weeks; some time

EXERCISE 5

1. (a) He doesn't live here now. **(b)** He still lives here. **2.** No difference. **3. (a)** They still work for the same company. **(b)** They don't still work for the same company. **4.** No difference. **5.** No difference.

EXERCISE 6

There are seven people staying in the hotel right now. B. Simpson has stayed there the longest.

1. ... stayed in the hotel for six nights. **2.** ... in the hotel since March 6. **3.** ... in the hotel since March 4. **4.** ... in the hotel for 10 nights. **5.** ... have stayed in the hotel for three nights. **6.** ... has stayed at the hotel since March 2. **7.** ... at the hotel for eight days/just over a week. **8.** ... at the hotel for three nights.

EXERCISE 7

1. He has worked for the TV station for eight years. **2.** They have been married since 1962. **3.** She has known how to fix a car for a long time. **4.** Since his car broke down, Tom has been riding his bike to work. **5.** I have wanted to go to China for several years. **6.** My brother hasn't smoked since he stopped smoking in college. **7.** I have been afraid of bats since I was a child. **8.** My mother has been in France since last week. **9.** My sister has been running two miles every morning since she was 15 years old. **10.** They have been going to Cape Cod every summer for 12 years.

EXERCISE 8

(2) for **(3)** have known **(4)** since **(5)** met **(6)** have worked **(7)** for **(8)** showed **(9)** taught **(10)** for **(11)** quit **(12)** haven't worked **(13)** since **(14)** started **(15)** ate

EXERCISE 9

Error in parentheses; corrections in italics.
6. (since) *for* **8.** (has found out) *found out* **10.** (takes) *has taken* **11.** (since) *for* Also possible: **3.** (several years) *for several years*

Activity 3

We recommend introducing this activity with a brief discussion of the system in the United States, based on the headings in the chart. If all your students come from the same country, this activity can be used as a research project. Students work in pairs or groups to choose one country and then research the relevant information outside class. In class, they follow the directions, using their research. The information that is shared and exchanged could be used as a written follow-up activity.

Activity 4

Check tapescript for answers.

Unit 14

Present Perfect and Simple Past

Ever and *Never*, *Already* and *Yet*

OPENING TASK

This task doesn't need much setting up since most students are familiar with passport stamps and recognize this right away.

Students work in pairs or groups.

Step 1: Check that everyone understands the two questions; **a)** is trickier than it looks. This should be treated as a problem-solving activity since it is not immediately apparent what the countries are. This is deliberate; it promotes discussion and genuine information exchange. Usually there is a least one person in the class who knows.

SOLUTION:
Step 1: (a) nine
(b): the UK (Heathrow, London) in 1996
France in 1992
Canada in 1990
Japan (Narita, Tokyo; Osaka) in 1995 and 1996
Taiwan/ROC (Republic of China) in 1995
Singapore in 1988
Indonesia in 1986
Malaysia in 1986
Thailand in 1986

Step 2:
(1) nine
(2) six
(3) Indonesia/Thailand
(4) 1986
(5) 1988
(6) 1986
(7) Japan
(8) 1995
(9) 1996
(10) 1995
(11) two
(12) France
(13) 1996
(14) Canada
(15) 1990

EXERCISE 1

1. Roman Holiday
Rest of answers will vary.

EXERCISE 2

2. Has Tom seen ...   3.Have Patty and Mark seen ...
4. Did Karen see ...last weekend?   5. Did Patty and

Mark see *Psycho*?   6. Has Robert seen *Psycho*?
7. Have Carolyn and Terry seen ...   8. Did Tom see the *Godfather* last night/yesterday/on Tuesday?

EXERCISE 3

(1) have walked   **(2)** have seen   **(3)** took   **(4)** went
(5) have seen   **(6)** went   **(7)** had   **(8)** have eaten
(9) tried   **(10)** have spent

EXERCISE 4

2. I've gone; *I went*   **3.** I've ridden; *I rode*   **4.** Have ever you been; *Have you ever been*   **5.** I've ever been; *I've been*   **6.** I've studied; *I studied*

EXERCISE 5

1. B I have/'ve never tried **B** I have/'ve never done **A** Have you ever washed **C** I have/'ve tried **A** did you try **C** I used
2. A Have you ever read **B** have; read **B** have/'ve forgotten; won
3. B Has he ever been **A** came **B** Has he been **A** he has/'s never been; he has traveled **B** Did you take **A** he has never visited
4. A Did you go out **B** We went **A** I have/'ve never been there **B** I have/'ve eaten **A** Have you ever tried **B** We had a

EXERCISE 6

Answers will vary, depending on students' experiences. Questions are likely to be similar: All will include *Have you ever ... (+ verb + past participle) ...?*

EXERCISE 7

(1) Have you eaten yet?   **(2)** Have you ever eaten/been/gone there?   **(3)** I never have/not yet
(4) Have you ever gone   **(5)** I never have   **(6)** Have you ever tried her cooking/eaten a dinner that she cooked   **(7)** Yes, I have   **(8)** I already did/stopped there

Activity 8

See tapescript for answers.

Unit 15

Present Perfect Progressive

OPENING TASK

Students work in pairs or groups to match the statements with an appropriate activity from the list in Step 2. There are more activities than statements to promote a little more discussion.

Step 1: Students read the statements and try to guess the context, speakers, and setting.

Step 2: Students match the activities to the statements. Bring the class together to see how much they agree/disagree. Students should be ready to justify their answers. You can elicit and/or weave in the fact that the statements refer to something that is apparent in the present and were caused by something that occurred before the present. This can act as a springboard to Focus 1. Exercise 1 returns to the task by getting students to write full sentences.

SOLUTION: Answers may vary. Accept anything that can be plausibly justified.

1. fixing a car   **2.** chopping onions   **3.** studying for a test   **4.** drinking   **5.** swimming   **6.** playing in the yard

EXERCISE 2

Answers will vary depending on the students' imaginations.
2. He has been kissing his girlfriend./He's been celebrating his birthday.   **3.** They have been shopping/spending money.   **4.** They have been hiking/walking for a long time.   **5.** She has been doing her homework /studying for a chemistry class.   **6.** She has been eating a hamburger with a lot of ketchup./She has been writing a letter with a red pen.   **7.** He has been playing with a cat/working in a circus or a zoo.

EXERCISE 3

2. have been writing   **3.** has been raining   **4.** has been barking   **5.** have been looking   **6.** have been living   **7.** have been studying   **8.** have been trying

EXERCISE 4

(2) 've been taking   **(3)** haven't been going   **(4)** 've been cooking/eating   **(5)** 've been feeling   **(6)** have you been doing?   **(7)** 've been seeing   **(8)** 've been sailing   **(9)** 've been spending   **(10)** 've been talking/thinking   **(11)** have you been doing   **(12)** 've been studying

EXERCISE 5

1. a   **2.** b   **3.** c   **4.** a   **5.** c

EXERCISE 6

1. I've been waiting for you to wake up for three hours.
2. I've been trying to change the oil for forty-five minutes.   **3.** We've been discussing it for ten years.
4. I've been planning dinner all day.

EXERCISE 7

(1) have/'ve been trying   **(2)** have been calling
(3) have/'ve been hoping   **(4)** Have you been waiting
(5) have you been   **(6)** have/'ve been standing
(7) has started   **(8)** started

Activity 4
See tapescript for answers.

Unit 16
Making Offers with *Would You Like*

OPENING TASK

The illustration itself sets up this one.

Students work in pairs if possible. You can have one group of three if there is an odd number of students in the class.

Step 1: You could make two lines, with all the As on one side of the room and all the Bs on the other so that the students really have to communicate across the room at some distance from each other. Check that students understand what they are to do. Make it clear that B has to communicate a solution to A's problem. You could demonstrate the first one for the students: You mime that you are thirsty. When someone understands the message, elicit an appropriate mimed "solution" to your problem.

Step 2: A and B students get back together to compare notes and to write solutions in the appropriate column. Again, you could model the first one if there is confusion.

Answers will vary.
1. Would you like something to drink?   2. Would you like an aspirin?   3. Would you like me to open the window?   4. Would you like me to get you something to eat?   5. Would you like a handkerchief?   6. Would you like a light and an ashtray?   7. Would you like a ride?   8. Would you like to dance?

You could have pairs take turns acting this out for the rest of the class.

Exercise 1 provides an opportunity for students to check the accuracy of their answers.

EXERCISE 1

Answers will vary.

EXERCISE 2

1. Would you like to ...   2. Would you like to ...
3. Would you like to ... coats?   4. Do you want/Would you like a chair?/... me to get you a chair?   5. Would you like ...   6. Do you want/Would you like ...
7. Would you like me to open the window for you?
8. Would you like more coffee?

EXERCISE 3

Answers will vary. All offers include *Would you like ...?* or *Do you want ...?* All refusals should include reasons for refusing.

EXERCISE 4

Answers will vary.
1. Would you like some more ... (coffee)...?   2. Would you like some more ... (soup/cake) ...?   3. Would you like to see ... (a photograph of something/my new ...)?
4. Would you like a blanket?/Would you like me to turn up the heat?   5. Would you like me to help you with that?/Would you like me to carry that for you?
6. Would you like to ...?   7. Would you like to borrow ...?

EXERCISE 5

Answers will vary. All offers include *Would ... like ...?* All positive responses should include *Thank you* or *Yes, please.* All refusals (except #6) should include reason for refusing and/or *Sorry, but ...* or *Thanks anyway ....*

Suggested offers:
1. Would you like me to turn the video on?   2. ... some more pie?   3. ... my seat?/... to sit here?   4. ... me to mail these for you?   5. ... a ride to work?   6. ... a ride?

Activities 1, 3, and 5

These charts are intended to provide a framework for students' "data collection" and notetaking. Students may want to redraw these on a larger piece of paper or in their notebooks so that there is more space for notes.

Activity 3

Check tapescript for answers.

Unit 17
Requests and Permission
Can/Could, Will/Would, May

OPENING TASK

Carefully explain the task situation here. You could act out what happened—how the coffee got spilled on the note—to show how difficult it is now to read everything clearly.

Students work in pairs or groups.

Step 1: Students read the note and try to guess what could go in the missing parts. They can write their guesses in the spaces in the note. You could bring the class together after Step 1 to provide an opportunity for students to compare their guesses thus far.

Step 2: Students read the actual missing parts and decide where they should go.

Bring the whole class together to check how much they agree. You could then elicit/weave in that in each sentence the writer is making a request. As a bridge to Focus 1 you could either make an overhead transparency of these requests or write them on the board and underline (or have the students underline) the parts of the sentence that show that the speaker is making a request.

SOLUTION: A 2 **B** 8 **C** 6 **D** 3 **E** 5 **F** 7 **G** 9 **H** 1 **I** 4

EXERCISE 1

Answers will vary.
1. Could you please tell me what time it is?   2. Could I have change for this dollar, please?   3. Would you mind holding my place in line?   4. Could you please move your chair?   5. Would you turn on the light, please?   6. Would you close the door, please?
7. Could you please speak a little more loudly?

EXERCISE 2

Students may want to redraw this chart on a larger piece of paper or in their notebooks so that there is more room for notetaking.

EXERCISE 3

Answers will vary.
1. Can you scratch my back?   2. Would you mind not smoking?   3. Can you move it a little more to the left/right?   4. Would you please take our picture?

EXERCISE 4

Request for Permission: 1, 3, 6, 8, 10, 11
General Request: 2, 4, 5, 7, 9

EXERCISE 5

Answers will vary. All requests and requests for permission include *Can ...?, Could ...?, Will ...?, Would ...?, May ...?*, and possibly *please* or *Would you mind ...?*
1. Would you mind if I handed in my assignment late?
2. May I close the window?   3. Can I ask a question, please?   4. May I speak to ...?   5. Can I talk to...?
6. Could I have a cookie?   7. May I have another ...?
8. May I help you?

EXERCISE 6

Answers will vary. All requests and requests for permission include *Can ...?, Could ...?, Will   ?, Would ...?, May ...?*, and possibly *please* or *Would you mind ...?*
Responses can be nonverbal or they can include short answers such as *Yeah, sure.* If requests for permission are refused, they should include a reason and/or *Sorry, but ...* or another "softening" phrase.

1. May I use the phone?   2. Could you repeat that, please?   3. Could you please tell me if Flight #255 from Denver is on time?   4. May I borrow your car?
5. Would you mind buying me some film?   6. May I leave the room now?   7. Can I/Would you shut the window, please?   8. Can you spare some time to talk with me?   9. Could I please change my appointment?   10. Can I have some tea?   11. May I hold your baby?

Activities 1 and 3

Students may want to redraw these charts on a larger piece of paper so that there is more room for notetaking.

Activity 5

Answers may vary slightly, but all should include a polite request and/or a request for permission.

Activity 6

Check tapescript for answers.

Unit 18

Used to with *Still* and *Anymore*

OPENING TASK

It would add a lot to this task if you could bring in a yearbook to set this in motion.

Students work in groups.

Step 1: Groups come up with as much information as they can about each person: Why is she/he famous? What do we know about him/her? If students don't know anything about any of these people, they should feel free to move around the room until they find someone who does. Often someone knows something about at least one of these people. Bring students together as a whole class to share what they found.

Step 2: Back in their groups, students match the pictures on page 269 with the pictures from their high school yearbooks.

Step 3: Groups decide who has changed the most and who has changed the least, giving reasons for their decisions. Bring the whole class together to share ideas from Step 3. Use this as a springboard for Focus 1. Exercises 1, 3, and 4 build on the task.

SOLUTIONS:
Step 1
Top row (l-r): Meryl Streep Madonna Diana Ross
Bottom row (l-r): Bruce Springsteen Tina Turner Michael Jackson

Step 2
Top row (l-r): Tina Turner Michael Jackson Diana Ross
Bottom row (l-r): Bruce Springsteen Meryl Streep Madonna

EXERCISE 1

1. Madonna didn't used to be a singer; she used to be a dancer. She used to be poor and she used to live in Michigan.   2. Bruce Springsteen used to have straight hair. He used to play football in high school. In addition, he used to live in New Jersey and he used to sing about blue-collar life.

EXERCISE 2

Answers will vary.

EXERCISE 3

Answers may vary.
1. Meryl Streep still has blond hair and she is still very slim. She still has the same smile. She still looks like she did in high school.   2. Bruce Springsteen still has a house in New Jersey and he is still called "The Boss".

EXERCISE 4

Answers will vary.

EXERCISE 5

1. anymore 2. still 3. still 4. anymore 5. still 6. still 7. anymore

EXERCISE 6

(2) used to grow fruit and vegetables   (3) used to mine silver in the north   (4) do not/don't mine it anymore (5) did not/didn't use to produce silk in the north (6) used to produce it in the south   (7) still mine diamonds in the southwest   (8) still grow coffee   (9) still mine gold

EXERCISE 7

always usually often sometimes seldom rarely hardly ever never

EXERCISE 8

Answers will vary.

Activity 5
Check tapescript for answers.

Unit 19

Past Perfect

Before and *After*

OPENING TASK

To set this task up, use the family tree in Step 1 to familiarize students not only with how a family tree works, but also with some of the key vocabulary. As a class, look at the family tree in Step 1 and make sure everyone can locate Tom. From here, briefly elicit/review vocabulary for family relationships. For example, "What relationship is Bernard to Tom?" "What relationship is Ann Ray to Tom?" "What relationship is Tom to Catherine Page?" and so on.

Students work in pairs.

Step 1: Explain that Tom left home to travel overseas and returned eight years later. The family tree in Step 1 shows his family when he left and the one in Step 2 shows his family when he returned.

Step 2: Pairs find how many ways his family changed while he was away by comparing the two family trees.

Step 3: Pairs write statements showing at least five of these changes.

SOLUTION: Number of changes in his family: 10
At the end of Step 3, you could bring the class together to see who found the most changes in Tom's family and to elicit the statements made in Step 3. On the basis of these statements, you could move to the information in Focus 1 and 2, as necessary. Exercise 1 then returns to the task with a focus on accuracy.

EXERCISE 1

2. had had two children   **3.** had (gotten) married three times/had (gotten) married and divorced three times   **4.** Tom got/arrived/returned home; had gotten married; had had a daughter   **5.** had had twin boys   **6.** lost her husband; had gained five great-grandchildren   **7.** had died when they were born   **8.** nephews; two nieces; three nephews   **9.** had become grandparents   **10.** had had; had not/hadn't (gotten) married; had (gotten) married; had not/hadn't had

EXERCISE 2

1. He took the bus because his car had broken down.
2. Charlotte was depressed because she had failed her English exam.   **3.** Tanya's skin was very red because she had sat in the sun all afternoon.   **4.** We were really hungry because we hadn't eaten all day.   **5.** Brenda's

clothes were too tight because she hadn't exercised for several months.   **6.** Neville couldn't sleep because he had drunk several cups of very strong coffee.   **7.** We thought the test was very easy because we had studied hard for three weeks.

EXERCISE 3

Sentences with checks: 2, 5, 7, 10

EXERCISE 4

1. Sue (had) studied several maps before she decided .../Before Sue decided ..., she (had) studied several maps.
2. She checked the tires on her bike after she (had) .../After she (had) changed ...   **3.** She (had) put fresh water in her bottle before .../Before she left home, she (had) put ...   **4.** She came to a very steep hill after she (had ridden)/rode .../After she (had ridden)/rode for several miles, she ...   **5.** She (had ridden)/rode to the top of the hill before she stopped .../Before she stopped to drink some water and enjoy the view, she (had ridden)/rode ...   **6.** She got a flat tire after she (had ridden) rode .../After she (had ridden) rode for ten more miles, she ...   **7.** She fixed the flat tire before she .../Before she continued her ride, she ...   **8.** She decided to go home after it (had) .../After it (had) started to rain, she ...   **9.** By the time she got home, she had ridden .../She had ridden over 30 miles by the time ...   **10.** She ate a huge plate of pasta after she (had taken)/took .../After she (had taken)/ took a long, hot shower, she ate ...

EXERCISE 5

1. because he *had eaten*   **2.** Jan *was* really confused   **3.** Graham *has* gone home   **4.** Howard *was* a lucky man/he *has* traveled   **5.** she *had broken* her leg   **6.** Before he *had left* the house   **7.** after she *has graded* them/Professor Westerfield always *returned*   **8.** your plane *had left*   **9.** they *had missed* the bus

EXERCISE 6

(2) graduated   **(3)** had made/made   **(4)** broke   **(5)** was painting   **(6)** lost   **(7)** did not/didn't go   **(8)** has not/hasn't visited   **(9)** has never been   **(10)** got   **(11)** had not/hadn't been   **(12)** came   **(13)** has met   **(14)** has not/hasn't been

Activity 1

Students may want to redraw this chart in their notebooks so that there is more room for notetaking.

Activity 3

To set this activity in motion, you could model it with events from American history, emphasizing that exact dates are not necessary. When students have completed their original charts, they can compile all their information on one big chart to create a shared point of reference. Students should redraw this chart so that it is big enough for the information collected.

Activity 5

Check tapescript for answers.

Unit 20

Articles

The, A/An, Some and ∅

OPENING TASK

To introduce the task, you could explain that it is about a couple, Esinam and Stuart, who are trying to buy a house. Feed in/elicit any vocabulary that you think your students might be unfamiliar with (for example, real estate agent, neighborhood, suburbs, remodel).

Students work in pairs or groups of three.

Step 1: Explain that all the sentences belong to the same story about Esinam and Stuart, but they are not in the correct order. Students decide on the order in which the sentences should go.

SOLUTION: f a i h c g d b e

Step 2: Explain that students need to look at the pictures and match the houses in the pictures with the houses in the story by numbering them according to the order in which they appear in the story.

SOLUTION: *Top row (l-r):* 1 2; *Center:* 5; *Bottom row (l-r):* 3 4

As a bridge to Focus 1, you could ask the students to explain how they came up with the order of sentences in Step 1. As they do so, you (or they) could underline the articles in the sentences on an overhead transparency or on the blackboard. From this, you could ask them to make generalizations about the use of *the* and *a*.

EXERCISE 1

1. a **2.** ∅ **3.** ∅ **4.** some **5.** a **6.** The **7.** a **8.** The **9.** the **10.** an **11.** ∅ **12.** ∅ **13.** a **14.** ∅

EXERCISE 2

1. a—singular count noun; talking about it (a doll) for the first time; answers the question *What?*

2. ∅—plural count noun; talking about a group of things (dolls), not a specific doll; answers the question *What?*
3. ∅—plural count noun; talking about a group of things (dolls), not a specific doll; answers the question *What?*
4. some—plural count noun; talking about quantity; answers the question *What??*
5. a—singular count noun; talking about it (a doll) for the first time; answers the question *What?*
6. The—singular count noun; second mention; answers the question *Which?*
7. a—singular count noun; talking about it (a baseball player's uniform) for the first time; answers the question *What?*
8. The—singular count noun; second mention; answers the question *Which?*
9. the—singular count noun; second mention; answers the question *Which?*
10. an—singular count noun; talking about it (an old doll) for the first time; answers the question *What?*
11. ∅—plural count noun; talking about a group of things (dolls), not a specific doll; answers the question *What?*
12. ∅—plural count noun; talking about presents; answers the question *What?*

EXERCISE 3

Correct: 1, 3, 5, 6, 7, 8, 9
Incorrect: **(2)** should use *the* because *orchard* has already been talked about   **(4)** should use *the* because *forest* has already been talked about   **(10)** should use *a* because this is the first time *deer-watching party* has been talked about

EXERCISE 4

1. a **2.** an; a **3.** a **4.** ∅; ∅; a **5.** ∅ **6.** ∅ **7.** ∅

Grammar Book Units

From Exercise 1:
2. can't use *some* with *dolls* because it is talking about *all* dolls (all members of a group of similar things)
3., 11., 12. same answer as **2.**

EXERCISE 6

1. an **2.** The **3.** the **4.** The **5.** an; a **6.** The **7.** some **8.** some **9.** the; the; the

EXERCISE 7

1. There should be no article before *love.* **2.** No article before *love.* **3.** No article before *money.* **4.** No article before *money.* **5.** No article before *health.* **6.** There should be an article before *Work.* **7.** There should be an article (the) before both *love* and *health.*

EXERCISE 8

Answers may vary.
1. (a) In a family's living room. **(b)** A parent or older sibling speaking to a younger child. **(c) Before** — the listener was near the TV. **After** — he or she turned on the TV. **2. (a)** In a family's living room. **(b)** A parent or older sibling speaking to a younger child. **(c) Before** — the listener was near the TV. **After** — he or she changed the channel. **3. (a)** In a classroom. **(b)** The teacher. **(c) Before** — the teacher ran out of chalk. **After** — a student did what was requested **4. (a)** In a garden. **(b)** A guest/visitor. **(c) Before** — they were taking a tour of the garden. **After** — they continued the tour. **5. (a)** At dinner. **(b)** One of the people at the table. **(c) Before** — they were serving themselves. **After** — someone honored the request. **6. (a)** In any public place. **(b)** A woman who needs to use the restroom. **(c) Before** — she was looking for the restroom or for someone to ask. **After** — the person she asked gave her directions. **7. (a)** In someone's house. **(b)** One family member to another (or roommate). **(c) Before** — they were discussing the weather or saying good-bye. **After** — the person said good-bye and left the house (without the umbrella). **8. (a)** In someone's home or outside in the yard. **(b)** One family member to another (or possibly a neighbor, if she or he doesn't own a dog). **(c) Before** — the person noticed the dog was gone. **After** — the other person answered the question and/or helped look for the dog. **9. (a)** Outside **(b)** Probably two people who are romantically involved, but not necessarily **(c) Before** and **after** - they made small talk and/or kissed **10. (a)** Anywhere **(b)** A family member **(c) Before** and **after** - they were discussing vacation plans and/or talking about mountains, beaches.

EXERCISE 9

1. a family's living room —L **2.** a family's living room —L **3.** a classroom —L, L **4.** a garden —L **5.** at dinner —L **6.** any public place —R **7.** in someone's house —U, L **8.** in someone's home outside in the yard —L **9.** outside —U **10.** anywhere —R, R **11.** in a family's house —L, L **12.** anywhere —R

EXERCISE 10

1. S —because *telephone booth* has been mentioned before.
2. R —because a related noun, *telephone booth*, has been mentioned before; *window* is part of the telephone booth.
3. R —because a related noun, *telephone booth*, has been mentioned before; all telephone booths have floors.
4. S —because *broom* has been mentioned before.
5. R —because a related noun, *telephone booth*, has been mentioned before; all telephone booths have telephones.
6. R —because a related noun, *telephone* and *telephone booth*, have been mentioned.
7. S —because *coffee mug* has been mentioned before.
8. S —because *phone call* has been mentioned before.

EXERCISE 11

h. the house - second mention **c.** The second place - because of the adjective *second;* the house - second mention **g.** the real estate agent - second mention; the house - second mention; the apartment buildings - second mention **d.** the end of a dead-end street - related mention (dead-end streets have an "end") *and* uniqueness because there is only one end of a dead-end street, which is regionally known **b.** the little house - second mention; the kitchen - second mention **e.** the kitchen - second mention; the house - second mention

EXERCISE 12

Answers may vary, since it may be possible to justify the choice of *the* for more than one reason.
line   1   the summer - f
line   2   the fire - b
line   3   the whole week - f
     3   the newspeople - b
     4   The Great Fires - b
     6   the shower - c, the soot - c and e
     7   the latest fire adventure - f, the fire coverage - c
     8   the news - b, the alarm - c
     9   the door - c, the sky - a
     11   The fire - d
     12   The smoke - e
     13   the highway - b, the fire - d

Answers may vary, since it may be possible to justify the choice of the or a for more than one reason.

a Personal Turn - not specific or identified; first mention

the forest - regionally known

a contract logger - not specific or identified; first mention

a job - not specific or identified; first mention

the Tyee Creek Fire - regionally known

the Hatchery Creek Fire - regionally known

a few years ago - not specific or identified; first mention

a densely wooded hillside - not specific or identified; first mention

the Blewett Pass Highway - regionally known

the Hatchery Fire base camp - regionally known and also related mention (base camp is related to large-scale fire-fighting efforts)

the U.S. Fish Hatchery - regionally known

the main fire - second mention and also the adjective *main* makes it "one of a kind" (there's only one main fire)

the camp - second mention

The Rat Creek Fire - regionally known

the base camp - second mention

a 16-hour shift - not specific or identified; first mention

a fireline - not specific or identified; first mention

The Rat Creek Fire - second mention and regionally known

the Leavenworth side of Mountain Home - the phrase makes it "one of a kind" (there's only one Leavenworth side)

the process - related mention (the process of the fire)

a swath - not specific or identified; first mention

the structures - related or second mention (*structures* = another word for *houses*

the electricity - universally known

the fire - second mention

the hill - related or second mention (*hill* = another word for *mountqin* in this context)

a backfire - not specific or identified; first mention

A helicopter - not specific or identified; first mention

a loudspeaker - not specific or identified; first mention

the bottom - regionally known (everyone can identify "which" bottom of the hill) and also related mention (*hills* have bottoms)

the orchard-bordered property - regionally known (everyone can identify "which" orchard-bordered property) and related or second mention (*property* = another word for *land*)

the fire - second mention

the hill - second mention

The surrounding woods - second or related mention (*woods* = another word for *forest*)

the house - second mention

the fire - second mention

the house - second mention

the right to sleep in his own bed - this phrase makes it "one of a kind" (Also could be considered universally known if we believe that all people have this right.)

Activity 5

The instructor could bring in another example (besides the one in the students' text) to help to set this in motion.

Activity 6

Check tapescript for answers.

Unit 21
Articles with Names of Places

OPENING TASK

The purpose of this task is to compare how many different answers people give, not to test geographical knowledge. Before starting, you could run over some of the vocabulary that you think your students might not know (for example, continent, desert, mountain range, planet).

Step 1: Students move around the room collecting answers until they have spoke to at least five different people. They should write down all the DIFFERENT answers that they get.

Step 2: Students get together with one or two people they have NOT spoken to yet and compare their answers to decide on the correct answers.

Step 3: Each group can record their answers in full sentence form (*The Amazon is the longest river.*) on a large piece of poster paper or newsprint. All the answers can be displayed on the walls and the students can walk around to compare answers, note any differences and which ones are right.

You can use these posters as a springboard for Focus 1, Exercise 1 returns to the task and focuses on accuracy.

EXERCISE 1

(A): 1. the Amazon   **5.** the Himalayas   **7.** the Sahara
8. the Pacific Ocean
(B) 2. Asia   **3.** Russia (previously the Soviet Union)
4. Australia (name of a country); Greenland   **6.** Mt. Everest   **9.** Lake Superior   **10.** Jupiter

EXERCISE 2

(1) ∅ **(2)** ∅ **(3)** ∅ **(4)** ∅ **(5)** ∅ **(6)** ∅ **(7)** the **(8)** the **(9)** the **(10)** ∅ **(11)** The **(12)** The **(13)** ∅

EXERCISE 3

Dialogue 1: **A.** the University of Washington
B. Louisiana State University   **A.** the South; the Pacific Northwest
Dialogue 2: **A.** Washington, D.C.   **B.** the White House; the Capitol; the Washington Monument   **A.** ∅   **B.** the Smithsonian; the National Gallery

EXERCISE 4

(1) ∅ **(2)** ∅ **(3)** the **(4)** the **(5)** ∅ **(6)** ∅ **(7)** the **(8)** ∅ **(9)** ∅ **(10)** the

EXERCISE 5

3. ∅ **4.** ∅ **5.** the **6.** the **7.** ∅ **8.** the **9.** the **10** ∅ **11** the **12.** the **13.** the **14.** ∅ **15** ∅ **16** ∅

EXERCISE 6

(2) the **(3)** ∅ **(4)** ∅ **(5)** ∅ **(6)** ∅ **(7)** the **(8)** ∅/the **(9)** the

EXERCISE 7

the Golden Gate Bridge   Asia
the Marin Headlands   Golden Gate Park
the East Bay   Kew Gardens
the Orient   the Asian Art Museum
Chinatown   the/∅ Strybring Arboretum
(Other places/tourist sites may be added, depending on what information students get from their classmates or teacher.)

Activity 4
Check tapescript for answers.

Unit 22

The Passive

OPENING TASK

Draw attention to the map of Campinilea and explain the task situation. Check that students know the compass points and check vocabulary as necessary (*wheat, copper, goats*, for example).

Students work in pairs or groups.

Step 1: Groups/pairs use the information from the map to match the activity with the location.

SOLUTION: grapes in the north   sheep in the northwest   cotton in the south   wheat in the east   copper in the southeast   goats in the west

Step 2: Pairs/groups write at least five sentences about the activities, showing where they take place. Each group could write its sentences on the board, on an overhead transparency, or on a large piece of newsprint or poster paper. Bring the class together to share and compare answers. Use the student-generated statements to draw attention to the information in Focus 1. Exercise 2 returns students to the sentences from Step 2 and focuses on accurate use of the passive. Exercises 2-4 extend and build on the information in the task.

EXERCISE 1

Answers depend on the sentences that students wrote in the opening task. It is likely that the passive will sound better since it is obvious who is performing the action (farmers, miners, etc.).

EXERCISE 2

1. 2   2. 1   3. 1   4. 2   5. 2   6. 1

Yes, because it is not important to know who performed the act (mining, planting, producing).

Rewritten statements: 2. *Silver has been mined throughout ....*   **3.** *The first crop of rice will be planted in ....*
6. Grapes have been produced in ...

EXERCISE 3

(1) was built   **(2)** are being   **(3)** will be finished
(4) was known   **(5)** were written   **(6)** were published
(7) are being translated   **(8)** is taught   **(9)** are spoken
(10) were arrested   **(11)** were robbed   **(12)** have been performed   **(13)** has been served   **(14)** have been invited

EXERCISE 4

The flowers were moved.   The door was opened, and the glass windowpane was broken.   The vase was taken.   The dresser drawer was opened, and a jewelry box was moved to the top of the dress.   Jewelry was stolen from the box.   The suitcase was moved and partially unlocked.   The telephone was unplugged/disconnected.

EXERCISE 5

1. (d) 2. (a) 3. (g) 4. (h) 5. (b) 6. (c) 7. (f) 8. (e)

EXERCISE 6

1. It will; get eaten.   2. getting fixed   3. got robbed; got taken.   4. got invited   5. 'll get stopped   6. are getting graded   7. got returned   8. will get published
9. didn't get paid   10. Did; get arrested

EXERCISE 7

4. got hit   5. got taken   7. will get published   8. got attacked   9. got damaged

EXERCISE 8

Passage 1: Unnecessary *by*-phrases to be crossed out: 2, 4, 5, 9

Passage 2: Unnecessary *by*-phrases to be crossed out: 1, 2, 3, 4, 5, 6, 7, 8, 9

EXERCISE 9

1. A baby got killed by ...   2. Elvis was seen ...   3. The vice president got kidnapped ...

4. Will Bill and Hillary get divorced?   The world's worst husband got married ...   6. A man's false teeth got stuck in his throat for ...

Activity 5
Check tapescript for answers.

Unit 23
Phrasal Verbs

OPENING TASK

This task is made up of five steps. You may want to bring the class together after each step to check on answers.

Students should work in pairs or in groups.

Step 1: Explain that the boy in the comic strip really, really, hates school. Pairs/groups try to guess what they think he is saying in each picture and how he feels. You could bring the class together after a few minutes to briefly share ideas thus far. Pairs/groups then go on to Step 2.

Step 2: Pairs/groups match the words from the comic strip with the "dictionary" definitions. Encourage them to make guesses.

SOLUTION: **(a)** mix up **(b)** goof up **(c)** looking up **(d)** shut up **(e)** listen up **(f)** hurry up **(g)** wake up **(h)** get up **(i)** throw up

You might want to bring the class together to share and compare answers before going on.

Step 3: Pairs/groups match Calvin's words with the pictures in the comic strip. Solution also on page AK-5.

SOLUTION: *Picture 1:* Wake up. Get up.
Picture 2: Shut up. Listen up. *Picture 3:* Throw up.
Picture 4: Mix up. Goof up. *Picture 5:* Hurry up.
Picture 6: Looking up.

Step 4: Answers will vary, of course. The purpose of the question is to have students think about why one variety of language might be used over another. Students may come up with responses like: Calvin is a young boy; the language is more conversational: informal and colloquial; the language shows his emotions: he feels very strongly about all these things.

Step 5: The purpose of this step is to elicit some language from students around the context of the task. Don't worry about accuracy or how many (if any) phrasal verbs are used. Exercise 1 returns to this step.

You might want to wrap up the task by asking students what they notice about everything Calvin says (to elicit the use of *up*) and to use this as a springboard to the information in Focus 1.

EXERCISE 1

Step 1: Answers depend on the sentences that students wrote in Step 5 of the opening task.

Step 2: Answers will vary. Some phrasal verbs likely to be used are: stand up, sit down, write down, look up, hand out, fill in, clean up, put down, help out.

EXERCISE 2

Answers will vary.

EXERCISE 3

(1) up **(2)** down **(3)** down **(4)** up **(5)** over **(6)** in **(7)** out **(8)** in **(9)** over **(10)** out **(11)** away

EXERCISE 4

Answers will vary.

EXERCISE 5

Answers will vary.
2. Would you mind reading over my letter to see if there are any mistakes?   3. Could you please tell my clients that I need to put off all my meetings and reschedule them next week?   4. I expect you to hand in your homework on time.   5. Can you hand out these fliers to students in the cafeteria?   6. I think you have got to talk this over with *him*.

EXERCISE 6

(2) put my boots on   **(3)** take them back   **(4)** find out **(5)** put it off   **(6)** called the store up   **(7)** threw those out   **(8)** try them on

EXERCISE 7

Answers to **C** will vary.
1) try on — in a clothing store   **2)** sit down — at a concert   **3)** check out — in a library   **4)** Turn up — at a party   **5)** get off —on a bus   **6)** hang up — on the telephone   **7)** put out/put all out — in an airplane **8)** set up/set a meeting up) — in an office

EXERCISE 8

2. call on her   **3.** ran into   **4.** get on   **5.** passed away **6.** find that out   **7.** put off   **8.** cheer Ron up

EXERCISE 9

Answers for incorrect placements only.

2. *Threw out* should stay together.   **3.** *Ran into* should stay together, since *run into* is inseparable.   **4.** *Call back* should stay together since *her* is a pronoun.
5. *Passed away* should stay together since *pass away* is inseparable.   **6.** *Went over* should stay together since *go over* is inseparable.

Answers may vary, depending on students' sentences in Exercise 5.

(2) come back   **(3)** eat out   **(4)** caught on   **(5)** ran into   **(6)** were getting off   **(7)** has grown up
(8) finding out   **(9)** turn down/turn the volume down

(10) came over   **(11)** talked it over   **(12)** putting on/putting headphones on   **(13)** come back
(14) show up

There are different ways to fill in the puzzle.
Step 1: Upper left: *off/up/out*
Lower left: *put/get/take; work/hold/get*
Upper right: *on; up*
Lower right: *look/put; put/get*

Step 2 would be a good dictionary skills activity, since students need to actually use each phrasal verb in a sentence.

Activity 3
Check tapescript for answers.

Unit 24
Adjective Clauses and Participles as Adjectives

OPENING TASK

This is another logical problem-solving task. Explain that there are four people: Lee, Tracy, Sid, and Kit, and the problem is to find out who loves whom. You could quickly read the clues aloud, and then draw attention to the chart. You could then model how to complete the chart by reading the first clue and having your students look at Lee's box and write: "the person who speaks French" on the line below "LEE loves...".

You could then elicit from the students where they should put the information in Clue 2. After that, put students in pairs or groups of three and let them solve the rest of the problem on their own.

SOLUTION: Also see page AK-5.

Information about Lee:
plays the piano
is a teacher
LEE
loves...
the person who speaks French
the writer
Name: SID

Information about Tracy:
is interested in history
runs 3 miles a day
is a doctor
TRACY
loves...
the person who tells amusing stories

the pilot
Name: KIT
Information about Kit:
tells amusing stories
is a pilot
KIT
loves...
the person that/who runs 3 miles a day
the doctor
Name: TRACY

Information about Sid:
speaks French
is a writer
SID
loves...
that/who plays the piano
the teacher
Name: LEE

You could draw the blank chart on the board or on an overhead transparency. When the students are ready, bring the class together and have them complete the chart for you. If necessary, draw attention to the way the adjective clauses add descriptive information.

Students will probably notice *the person that plays the piano* in Clue 5 and *the person who plays the piano* in Clue 8. Both *that* and *who* are also in Clues 7 and 12. You can use this to point out that *who* and *that* both refer to people, and to make a bridge to the information in Focus 1. In Exercise 1, students return to the task to apply this information.

Adjective clause is underlined; relative pronoun is italicized and noun it describes is in parentheses.
1. Lee loves the (person) *who* speaks French. **O**
2. Tracy loves the (person) *who* tells amusing stories. **O**
3. No adjective clauses.
4. The pilot loves the (person) *who* is interested in history. **O**
5. Sid loves the (person) *that* plays the piano. **O**
6. The (person) *who* tells amusing stories is a pilot. **S**
7. The (person) *that* runs three miles a day is a doctor. **S**
8. The (person) *who* plays the piano is a teacher. **S**
9. The (person) *who* is interested in history is a doctor. **S**
10. The doctor loves the (person) *who* tells amusing stories. **O**
11. The (person) *who* speaks French is a writer. **S**
12. The pilot loves the (person) *who* runs three miles a day. **O**

EXERCISE 2

Answers will vary, depending on what information students use. It may be helpful to have students check their answers with each other to see if they are factually correct and also to make sure that students can identify adjective clauses, relative pronouns, and the nouns they describe.

EXERCISE 3

This will depend on what information the students in the class give each other.

EXERCISE 4

Content will vary. Appropriate relative pronouns are: *who* or *that* for people, *which* or *that* for things (non-humans).

EXERCISE 5

There may be some variety in how this passage is rewritten. The following is one way:

It's interesting talking with women who have had experiences which are similar to mine since there are a lot of things to talk about. For example, *balance* is a topic which most of my women friends are interested in, since achieving balance is a challenge for many women who have jobs and family responsibilities.
Women who don't have jobs outside of their homes sometimes feel criticized by other people who think that women should have careers. This is an attitude which more and more people share.
Women who work at jobs and have young children also feel criticized by other people who think that all women should stay at home with their children. Some people believe that children should never be sent to a day care center, which is a business, not a loving home. This is a belief which makes some women feel a lack of balance in their lives.
Women who never have children may feel pressure from their own parents, who worry that their children won't provide them with grandchildren. These are examples that show how it can be difficult for women to feel sure they are doing the right thing for themselves and for their children.

EXERCISE 6

Order of answers: Left to right, down the page.

embarrassing rip, embarrassed man; rip → man   disgusting eating habits, disgusted woman; man → woman   surprised woman, surprising gift; woman ← flowers   shocked man, shocking haircut; man ← woman   confusing map, confused man; map → man   stimulating conversation/discussion, stimulated woman; discussion → woman   interested woman, interesting flower arranging; woman ← flower arranging   amusing comics, amused man; comics → man   inspired man, inspiring view; man ← view

EXERCISE 7

1. annoying   2. comforting   3. frightening   4. relaxing / soothing   5. frightened   6. amusing   7. boring   8. surprising   9. amusing   10. exciting   11. shocking   12. entertaining   13. disappointed

EXERCISE 8

interested should be ***interesting***
unexpected, stimulating — OK
surprised should be ***surprising***
shocked — OK
embarrassing should be ***embarrassed***
disgusting — OK
inspired, talented — OK; *amused* should be ***amusing***
bored should be ***boring***

Activity 4
Check tapescript for answers.

Unit 25

Conditionals

OPENING TASK

You could use the task illustration to check whether everyone understands "desert island" and to explain the task situation. Make sure that everyone can identify the objects and emphasize that the woman in the illustration is imagining the situation.

Students work in pairs or groups of three.

Step 1: Students complete the sentences as shown. Answers will vary.

Step 2: Students share and compare their ideas and vote on the most interesting and creative ones. They could write these on the board and you could then draw upon their own ideas to introduce the information in Focus 1. Exercise 1 returns to the task, giving students the opportunity to review what they wrote in Step 2 and to revise it as necessary.

EXERCISE 1

Step 1: Answers will depend on what students wrote in the opening task.

Step 2: Answers will vary.

EXERCISE 2

Answers will vary. Main clauses should all use *would*.

EXERCISE 3

Answers will vary, but main clauses should all use *would*, and *if* clauses should be based on the previous main clause.

EXERCISE 4

2. He is not rich, so he can't afford to go out to eat all the time or never have to cook at home. *were; would; would* **3.** He can't buy anything he wants because he's not rich. *would; were* **4.** He doesn't have a girlfriend, so he can't buy her anything she wants. *had; would*

Sentences 5-8: It is difficult to state what is not true about each sentence, since these are all based on the Sandira's fantasy about having a girlfriend. But if we suppose he **does** have a girlfriend:

5. His girlfriend doesn't want to buy more and more, since he doesn't buy her whatever she wants. *bought; would* **6.** She hasn't run out of things to buy, since she doesn't/isn't able to buy more and more. *bought; would*

7. Since she hasn't run out of things to buy, she has not fallen out of love with Sandira. *would; ran* **8.** He isn't miserable because she hasn't fallen out of love with him. *fell; would* **9.** He doesn't go to the movies every week because he isn't miserable. *were; would*

EXERCISE 5

Answers are likely to include the following, but students may find even more than these:

Examples: If Ilene hadn't received a party invitation, she wouldn't have gone out on New Year's Eve. If Jeff had been gay, he wouldn't have been interested in Ilene.

If Diane hadn't persuaded Ilene to change her mind, she wouldn't have gone to the party.

If Ilene hadn't left the party invitation at home, she wouldn't have ended up at the party where she met Jeff.

If Ilene had remembered the right address, she wouldn't have ended up at the party where she met Jeff.

If Diane hadn't persuaded Ilene to stay at the party, she might have left before she met Jeff.

If Ilene hadn't tripped down the steps, she wouldn't have been caught in Jeff's arms.

If Jeff hadn't been visiting his sister next door, he wouldn't have gone next door to the party at all.

If Jeff hadn't gone next door to tell people to turn the music down, he wouldn't have met Ilene.

If there hadn't been a terrible snowstorm that night, he would have been in West Africa.

If Jeff had stayed in West Africa longer, he might have forgotten about Ilene.

EXERCISE 6

Answers will vary.

EXERCISE 7

2. knew/had known; would have changed **3.** got; would not be **4.** would run away; yelled **5.** had; would buy **6.** had not learned; would have been **7.** had not rained; would have remembered **8.** would be able; rained

EXERCISE 8

Answers will vary.

EXERCISE 9

1. c   2. g   3. f   4. a   5. b   6. d   7. e

EXERCISE 10

Answers will vary.

EXERCISE 11

1. future (probable)   2. hypothetical (improbable)
3. hypothetical (improbable)   4. hypothetical
(improbable)   5. future (probable)   6. future (probable)   7. hypothetical (improbable)   8. hypothetical (improbable)

EXERCISE 12

2. Gao's wife really might change careers, so the *if*-clause might be true. The future conditional can be used: *changes; will study to be a...(lawyer/writer, etc.)*   3. The *if*-clause cannot be true because Antonieta lives in New Zealand. The counterfactual conditional must be used: *had stayed; would not be*   4. Antonieta may move to France next year, so the *if*-clause might be true. The future conditional can be used: *will speak French; moves*
5. Mary's car really might break down since it is old. The future conditional can be used: *breaks down; will need ... (to fix it/to buy a new car, etc.)*   6. The *if*-clause cannot be true because Mary has a car. The counterfactual conditional must be used: *didn't have; would have to..(ride the bus/buy one)*   7. The future conditional can be used since the *if*-clause may be true—Marcia might actually be accepted into graduate school: *will start; gets*   8. Since Mary raised a family instead of going to school, the *if*-clause cannot be true. The counterfactual conditional must be used: *had continued; would have begun*

EXERCISE 13

Answers may vary.
1. if you pet them   2. if you heat it   3. whenever it is warm   4. when you spill it   5. if the temperature is below 0° Celsius/32° Fahrenheit   6. it will turn on
7. if you heat it   8. if they like the play

EXERCISE 14

There may be some variation in answers, but they are likely to be the following:
(1) will/'ll go camping   (2) might visit   (3) might stay
(4) will/'ll break   (5) will/'ll spill   (6) wouldn't have won   (7) wouldn't be rich   (8) wouldn't have
(9) would have gone back   (10) would have won

Activity 1
Students may want to redraw this chart on a larger piece of paper so that there is more room.

Activity 7
Check tapescript for answers.

Grammar Dimensions Book 2

Name _____

Unit 1: Simple Present Habits, Routines, and Facts

Score _____
100

SECTION A
Circle the letter of the *incorrect* underlined word or phrase.

1. Allison (A) <u>plays</u> the violin in an orchestra and (B) <u>sometimes</u> (C) <u>give</u> private lessons.

2. She (A) <u>hardly never</u> (B) <u>works</u> in the morning and she (C) <u>enjoys</u> sleeping late.

3. She (A) <u>usually</u> (B) <u>wears</u> a black dress for concerts but she (C) <u>don't wear</u> a uniform.

4. She (A) <u>drinks</u> some coffee and (B) <u>she always eat</u> a sandwich before the concert (C) <u>begins.</u>

5. (A) <u>Sometimes she walks</u> home, but she (B) <u>rides usually</u> the bus. She (C) <u>doesn't ever take</u> taxis.

SECTION B
Philip is a high school English teacher. He's talking to his friend Ann about how he spends his lunch period at school. Complete what he says using verbs that will complete the meaning. Sometimes more than one answer is possible.

Ann: What **(6)**_____ (you usually) for lunch?

Philip: We **(7)**_____ (not) much time to eat and I **(8)**_____ (not) to spend

much money on lunch, so I usually **(9)** _____ sandwiches from home.

Ann: **(10)**_____ you ever _____ lunch in the school cafeteria?

Philip: No, I hardly ever **(11)**_____ there, but my friend Tom always

(12)_____ his lunch there and he **(13)**_____ the food is pretty good.

Ann: **(14)**_____ all of the students _____ in the cafeteria?

Philip: No. A lot of them **(15)**_____ lunch outdoors.

SECTION C
Complete the sentence with one of these frequency adverbs (*always, usually, sometimes, never*) to make the sentence true. Sometimes more than one answer is possible.

16. Cats and dogs don't _____ get along with each other.

17. Animals _____ escape from zoos.

18. The sun _____ rises in the west.

19. It _____ sets in the west.

20. Bears _____ sleep a lot in the winter.

SECTION D
Write a sentence about something you usually do on your birthday.

21._____.

Write a sentence about something you never do in your English class.

22._____.

Choose an animal and write two sentences about its habits.

23. _____.

24. _____.

Write a sentence about something that a lot of people do in hot weather.

25._____.

UNIT 1 ANSWERS

A. **1.** C **2.** A **3.** C **4.** B **5.** B

B. **6.** do...have/eat **7.** don't have **8.** don't like **9.** bring **10.** Do...have/eat **11.** eat
12. has/eats **13.** says **14.** Do...eat **15.** have/eat

C. **16.** usually **17.** sometimes **18.** never **19.** always **20.** always/usually

D. 21.-25. Sentences will vary.

Grammar Dimensions Book 2

Unit 2: Present Progressive and
Simple Present Actions and States

Name _____

Score _____
100

SECTION A

Look around you in the classroom. Write two sentences about what's happening right now.

1. _____.

2. _____.

Think of some people (friends or family members) who are not in your English class. What are

they probably doing at the moment? Write two sentences.

3. _____.

4. _____.

What are you wearing today? Write a complete sentence.

5. _____.

SECTION B

Check the sentence a) or b) that is closest in meaning to the first statement or pair of statements.

6. A: John's eating a lot these days.

   B: I know. He's getting ready to run the marathon.

   a) He doesn't usually eat so much.   b) John always has a big appetite.

7. My parents are staying in a hotel.

   a) They live in a hotel.   b) They plan to leave in a few days.

8. Isabel teaches history at the community college.

   a) She's in class right now.   b) She has a job at the community college.

9. Great! We're going out for dinner tonight!

   a) We go out for dinner every night.   b) We seldom go out for dinner.

10. Andrew's really tired this semester. He's driving a taxi.

    a) His last job was easier.   b) He's working right now.

SECTION C

Complete the following using either the simple present or the present progressive. Use the words in parentheses.

A: Where **(11)**_____ you _____ (go) in this awful weather?

B: To class. The teacher **(12)**_____ (give) a review for next week's test.

C: Where's Kim?

D: He **(13)**_____ (take) a nap on the porch right now. He **(14)**_____ (not

sleep + usually) very well at night.

E: Most of my friends **(15)**_____ (study) in the library, but I

(16) _____ (study + always) better at home.

F: Not me. My brother and sister **(17)**_____ (make) too much noise.

G: There's Meredith. See? She **(18)**_____ (eat) soup and **(19)**_____ (read)

the newspaper.

H: She **(20)**_____ (read) everywhere. How can she concentrate?

SECTION D

Complete the following with the simple present or the present progressive, using the words in parentheses.

Marjorie **(21)**_____ (not like + usually) detective stories, but she

(22)_____ (love) the one she **(23)**_____ (read) now. With most books, she

(24)_____ (know) who's guilty after the first few chapters, but this time she

(25)_____ (have) trouble solving the mystery.

UNIT 2 ANSWERS

A. **1. - 5.** Students' own sentences.

B. **6.** a
7. b
8. b
9. b
10. a

C. **11.** are...going
12. is giving
13. is taking
14. doesn't usually sleep
15. study
16. always study
17. make
18. is eating
19. reading
20. reads

D. **21.** doesn't usually like
22. loves
23. is reading
24. knows
25. is having

Grammar Dimensions Book 2

Unit 3: Talking About the Future *Be going to* and *Will*

Name _____

Score _____
100

SECTION A
You visit a fortune teller. He predicts some good things about your future, and some things that don't make you very happy. Match the two parts of his predictions by writing the correct letter in the space after each number. Don't use any part more than once.

1. You will have   **A.** to live to be 100 years old.

2. You're going to   **B.** have more than two children.

3. You won't   **C.** an interesting life.

4. You'll learn to   **D.** make a lot of money.

5. You're not going   **E.** speak English perfectly.

SECTION B
Complete these sentences with will or be going to. Sometimes both forms are possible.

A: The weather report says it **(6)**_____ snow.

B: Cool! Do you think they **(7)**_____ close the schools?

A: Do you think people **(8)**_____ carry passports fifty years from now?

B: I don't know, but I think it **(9)**_____ be easier to travel from one country to another.

A: So, Doctor, what **(10)**_____ happen if I don't take this medicine?

B: Your condition **(11)**_____ get much worse.

A: What's all that lumber doing in your garage? What **(12)**_____ (you) build?

B: I **(13)**_____ make some shelves for my son's room.

I don't believe it! That guy **(14)**_____ take that parking space, and I was here first!

I **(15)**_____ be exactly twice your age in five more years.

SECTION C
Use will or be going to.

Write two predictions about a friend's future.

16. _____.

17. _____.

Write two sentences about things you intend to do this weekend.

18. _____.

19. _____.

Write a sentence about something you don't intend to do this weekend.

20. _____.

SECTION D
Complete the following sentences using be going to, will or 'll as appropriate.

A: It's freezing in here!

B: Hold on! I **(21)**_____ close the window.

I **(22)**_____ make coffee. Do you want a cup?

What time **(23)**_____ (you) leave for the airport?

I **(24)**_____ be glad to help you if you have any questions.

May I borrow this book? I promise I **(25)**_____ bring it back next week.

UNIT 3 ANSWERS

A. **1.** C **2.** D (B) **3.** B (D) **4.** E **5.** A

B. **6.** is going to **7.** will **8.** will **9.** will **10.** will/is going to
11. will/is going to **12.** are you going to **13.** 'm going to
14. is going to **15.** 'll

C. **16.- 20.** Students' own sentences.

D. **21.** 'll **22.** 'm going to **23.** are you going to **24.** 'll **25.** 'll

Grammar Dimensions Book 2

Unit 4 Asking Questions
Yes/No, Wh-, Tag Questions

SECTION A
Write an appropriate question word in the space provided.

1. A: _____ cut your hair? B: Why? Don't you like it?

2. A: _____ do your exams begin? B: In about three weeks.

3. A: _____ of these coats is yours? B: Neither.

4. A: _____ has everybody gone? B: Don't ask me. I just got here myself.

5. A: _____ didn't you take the bus? B: I forgot my pass.

SECTION B
Put the words in the correct order to form the appropriate questions.

6. A: (start/skiing/did/when/you) _____?

B: I was so young that I can't remember.

7. A: (did/how long/you/it take/learn/to) _____?

B: It didn't take me long at all.

8. A: (you/bones/have/ever/any/broken) _____?

B: Just this one.

9. A: (to/ski/have/favorite/you/place/do/a) _____?

B: Wherever there's snow.

10. A: (teach/could/me/to/you/ski) _____?

B: Sure, but it will take some time.

SECTION C
In the blank below, write the question that would give you the following answers.

We had such a great weekend. We visited friends who have a farm about two hundred miles from here.

11. _____.

By train. We were going to drive there, but we were both too tired on Friday afternoon. Our friends picked us up at a little station about ten miles from their farm.

12. _____.

Oh, they only grow enough vegetables to feed themselves. It's a pretty small place.

13. _____.

I don't know. Probably not more than ten acres, but it's beautiful and very quiet.

14. _____.

We got back late Sunday night, and we were so glad we didn't have to fight traffic!

15. _____.

They're coming to see us at Thanksgiving.

SECTION D
Complete the following statements with an appropriate question tag.

16. You both liked the restaurant, _____?

17. He'll be thirty next month, _____?

18. The test was awful, _____?

19. They speak French in Haiti, _____?

20. Chickens can't fly, _____?

21. You haven't seen Gabriel today, _____?

22. Lisa can use a computer, _____?

23. They weren't late to class, _____?

24. Rain smells great, _____?

25. He won't be here tomorrow, _____?

UNIT 4 ANSWERS

A. **1.** Who   **2.** When   **3.** Which   **4.** Where   **5.** Why

B. **6.** When did you start skiing?   **7.** How long did it take you to learn?
8. Have you ever broken any bones?   **9.** Do you have a favorite place to ski?
10. Could you teach me to ski?

C. **11.** How did you get there?   **12.** What do they grow on the farm?   **13.** How big is it?
14. When did you get back?   **15.** When are they coming to visit you?/When are you going to
see them again?

D. **16.** didn't you   **17.** won't he   **18.** wasn't it   **19.** don't they   **20.** can they
21. have you   **22.** can't she   **23.** were they   **24.** doesn't it   **25.** will he

Grammar Dimensions Book 2

Unit 5 Modals of Probability and Possibility

Name _____

Score _____
    100

SECTION A
Fill in the blank with the simple form of the verb in parentheses or with *could, might, must,* or *may* and the verb.

A: Does John speak Vietnamese? I know he was born in the U.S.

B: His last name is Nguyen, so he **(1)**_____ (speak) it.

C. Not necessarily, but I know that his grandmother **(2)**_____ (not understand) much

   English, and he's very close to her. So, he **(3)**_____ (speak) it.

D: I have no idea what to get Suzy for her birthday.

E: You **(4)**_____ (give) her a house plant.

D. No, I don't think I've ever seen a plant in her apartment. She **(5)**_____ (have) some

   kind of allergy or she **(6)**_____ (not like) them.

F: You teach math at Central High? So does my brother!

G: Well, I **(7)**_____ (know) him then.

H: Whose book is this? It was left in the school cafeteria.

I: It **(8)**_____ (belong) to anyone.

H: Well, not any of the kids, but it **(9)**_____ belong to a teacher or one of the office

   staff.

I: Wait, it has Muriel's initials in it and I know she loves this author. It **(10)**_____ be

   hers.

SECTION B
Check the statement which best describes the situation.

11. The bumper sticker on the car in front of you says, "I brake for animals."
   a. Someone who uses the car must be a veterinarian.
   b. Someone who uses the car could be a veterinarian.
   c. Someone who uses the car is a veterinarian.

12. George always stops for a few drinks after work and often gets into fights. Sometimes at the office his breath smells of alcohol. The police stopped him last week for drunk driving and took away his license.
   a. George might have a drinking problem.   b. George must have a drinking problem.
   c. George has a drinking problem.

13. You know that Walter takes singing lessons every week and practices every day. He sings in a church choir on Sunday and in a choral group on Wednesdays. You've never heard him sing.

    a. Walter may sing very well.   b. Walter must sing very well.   c. Walter sings very well.

14. Alex and Carol were robbed three times last year, so they've decided to sell their house. They spend very little time at home now, and they've started looking at apartments.

    a. They may want to move.   b. They must want to move.   c. They want to move.

15. Mike always turns down invitations to go to the beach. If he's near a pool, he's always fully dressed and usually says he's getting a cold and can't go in the water.

    a. He may not know how to swim.   b. He must not know how to swim.

    c. He doesn't know how to swim.

SECTION C
You find a small black bag on the ground. Write five thoughts you have about the person who lost it, based on the items you find in the bag. Use *could, might, may* or *must* to show how certain you feel.

16. a pack of cigarettes, matches, and some breath mints_____.

17. a business card that reads, "Miguel Guerra, insurance broker."_____.

18. a tape measure_____.

19. a computer diskette_____.

20. a tiny pair of scissors_____.

SECTION D
Fill in the blanks with *could have, might have, must have* or *may have.*

21. David was out late last night and he's not in class today. He _____ overslept again.

22. I walked home alone at two o'clock in the morning.

Are you crazy? You _____ been killed.

23. What's Steve's degree in ?

Steve _____ studied economics; I'm not sure.

24. I really put my foot in my mouth. You _____ told me that Ben and Yoko had broken up.

25. Who ate the last of the cheesecake?

It _____ been your brother. He's got a key to this apartment.

UNIT 5 ANSWERS

A. **1.** must/may **2.** doesn't understand **3.** may/must **4.** could **5.** may/might
6. might/may **7.** must **8.** could **9.** may/might **10.** must

B. **11.** b **12.** c **13.** b **14.** b **15.** a

C. **16.** He must be a smoker./He must smoke.
17. He may be Miguel Guerra or he may know someone named Miguel Guerra.
18. He could be a tailor or a carpenter.
19. He must use a computer.
20. He may use them to cut his nails./They might be for cutting out newspaper articles.

D. **21.** may have **22.** could have **23.** might have **24.** could have/might have
25. must have

Grammar Dimensions Book 2

Name _____

Unit 6 Past Progressive and Simple Past with Time Clauses *When, While,* and *As Soon As*

Score _____
100

SECTION A
Match the parts of these sentences by writing the correct letter in the space after the number.

1. When I was studying last night   **A.** I was still trying to catch the cat.

2. My cat was sitting in my lap while   **B.** the firefighters turned off the alarm.

3. As soon as the alarm rang   **C.** the fire alarm went off.

4. When the fire truck arrived   **D.** I was working on a math problem.

5. I was carrying him out of the building when **E.** he ran under the bed.

SECTION B
Check the sentence (a) or (b) closest in meaning to the statement.

6. The alarm rang at the fire station while the fire fighters were playing cards.

 (a) The firefighters finished their game before the alarm rang.

 (b) The firefighters started playing cards before the alarm rang.

7. As soon as the alarm sounded, some of them started putting on their gear.

 (a) They put on their gear after the alarm sounded.

 (b) The alarm sounded after they started putting on their gear.

8. The captain was shouting instructions while they were getting into the truck.

 (a) He was shouting and the firefighters were getting into the truck at the same time.

 (b) After the firefighters got into the truck, the captain began to shout.

9. When the fire truck arrived, people were running out of the building.

 (a) People ran out after the fire truck arrived.

 (b) People started to run out before the fire truck arrived.

10. As soon as they put out the fire, the firefighters turned off the alarm.

 (a) The alarm was ringing when they put the fire out.

 (b) The alarm stopped ringing before they put the fire out.

SECTION C
Janet and Fred were out walking the dog when the alarm went off, so they missed the excitement. They're talking to one of their neighbors outside their apartment building. Use the simple past or past progressive to fill in the blanks.

Steve: It was so stupid. I **(11)**_____ (heat) a pizza in the oven. It's all my fault.

Fred: What **(12)**_____ (you) (do) when you **(13)**_____ (hear) the alarm?

(14)_____ (you) (sleep)?

Steve: No, I **(15)**_____ (watch) T.V. and I **(16)**_____ (think) the noise was

part of the program.

Janet: What **(17)**_____ (you) (do) when you **(18)**_____(realize) it was the

fire alarm?

Steve: As soon as I **(19)**_____ (smell) the smoke, I **(20)**_____ (run) into the

kitchen.

SECTION D
Some other people are standing in front of the building, too. Write sentences using the simple past and the past progressive to describe what they were doing and what they did when the alarm went off.

(A man holding a crying baby and the baby's bottle)

21. _____ when _____.

22. As soon as _____, _____.

(A man with paint on his hands and clothes, with a woman holding a book and a pair of glasses)

23. _____ while _____

(A woman with wet hair wearing a bathrobe and holding a cat)

24. _____ when_____

25. _____ as soon as_____.

UNIT 6 ANSWERS

A. **1.** C **2.** D **3.** E **4.** A **5.** B

B. **6.** b **7.** a **8.** a **9.** b **10.** a

C. **11.** was heating **12.** were you doing **13.** heard **14.** were you sleeping
15. was watching **16.** thought **17.** did you do **18.** realized **19.** smelled **20.** ran

D. **21.** He was feeding the baby when the alarm went off.
22. As soon as the alarm went off, he ran out of his apartment.
23. He was painting while she was reading.
24. She was washing her hair when the alarm went off.
25. She got out of the shower and got her cat as soon as she heard the alarm.

Grammar Dimensions Book 2

Name _____

Unit 7 Similiarities and Differences, Comparatives, Superlatives, *As .. A, Not As .. As*

Score _____
100

SECTION A

There are five children in the Smith family. Their ages and heights are as follows:

Albert	Paula	Stephanie	Anthony	Virginia
23	21	21	18	16
5'10"	5'8"	5'8"	6'0"	5'11"

Complete the following statements with a comparative, a superlative, or an expression of similarity or difference.

1. Anthony is six feet tall. He's _____ of the five children.

2. The twins, Paula and Stephanie, are not _____ Virginia, who's 5'11".

3. Virginia is 16 years old. She's the _____.

4. Paula was born before Stephanie. She's two minutes _____ her twin.

5. Albert is two inches _____ Anthony.

6. Paula and Stephanie are the _____ of the five children.

7. Albert is the _____ child.

8. Anthony is three years _____ the twins.

SECTION B

Correct the mistake in each of the following statements.

9. All the Smith children are just active and intelligent as their parents.

10. Stephanie is probably the more outgoing member of the family.

11. Paula is anywhere near as friendly as her sister.

12. The twins don't study as much as their brothers, but they make the best grades than the boys.

13. Virginia is very athletic. She plays a lot more sports than her sisters are.

14. Anthony is a little shy. He doesn't have as many friends like Stephanie.

15. Stephanie can sing, but she can't play a musical instrument. She's probably the less musical of

the Smith children.

SECTION C
Write sentences in which you compare yourself to a member of your family, a friend, or a famous person. Use *as.....as* and *not as ..... as* one time each.

16. _____ (tall)

17. _____ (old)

18. _____ (smart)

19. _____ (athletic)

20. _____ (creative)

SECTION D
Re-write the following sentences so that they are less direct and more tactful.

21. Anthony is stupider than his brother._____.

22. Albert is shorter than Anthony. _____.

23. Paula and Stephanie work hard. Virginia works less than her sisters._____.

24. Albert is the ugliest of the Smith children._____.

25. Virginia is poorer than her brothers and sisters._____.

UNIT 7 ANSWERS

A. **1.** the tallest   **2.** as tall as   **3.** youngest   **4.** older than   **5.** shorter than   **6.** shortest   **7.** oldest   **8.** younger than

B. **9.** .. are just <u>as</u> active and intelligent   **10.** . . . the <u>most</u> outgoing member
   11. Paula is <u>not</u> anywhere near   **12.** ...they make <u>better</u> grades than
   13. ... than her sisters <u>do</u>.   **14.** . . .as many friends <u>as</u> Stephanie   **15.** ... the <u>least</u> musical

C. **16. - 20.** Students' own sentences.

D. **21.** Anthony is not as intelligent as his brother.
   22. Albert is not as tall as Anthony.
   23. Virginia doesn't work as hard as her sisters.
   24. Albert isn't as good-looking as his brothers and sisters.
   25. Virginia doesn't have as much money as her brothers and sisters.

Grammar Dimensions Book 2

Unit 8: Measure Words

SECTION A

You need to go grocery shopping. The only food items you have in your kitchen are the following. What quantity do you have of each? Write a measure word or expression in the space next to the number. Also, circle C (count noun) or NC (non-count noun) next to each item as appropriate.

1. _____ mayonnaise   C   NC

2. _____ apples   C   NC

3. _____ crackers   C   NC

4. _____ lettuce   C   NC

5. _____ coffee   C   NC

SECTION B

You feel like making and eating a big breakfast. Write the names of the foods you buy.
Example: a box of <u>pancake mix</u>.

6. a carton of _____   **7.** a box of _____

8. a jar of_____   **9.** a loaf of _____

10. a pound of_____

SECTION C

Re-write each of these sentences to have the same general meaning, using one of the following words or phrases: *most, a few, none, a little, a lot of.*

11. Every friend I have hates lima beans._____.

12. There are dozens of peaches here. Five or six are green._____.

13. I have twelve brothers and sisters. Eleven are allergic to chocolate._____.

14. They spent $1000 last month, $300 last week, and $400 this week at the

supermarket._____.

15. She can count to 100, say 'hello', 'please', and 'thank you', ask for directions, and order a meal

in Greek._____.

SECTION D

Fill in the blank with the letter of the most suitable word or phrase.

16. I don't like to go shopping when there are _____ people in the supermarket.

   a. most   b. a lot   c. many

17. I prefer to go very early on Saturday morning, when _____ the produce is really fresh.

    a. some   b. all   c. a great deal

18. _____ shoppers are very agressive, and move through the aisles very quickly.

    a. few of   b. several of   c. some

19. If you have very _____ items—no more than ten—you can go to the express check-out lane.

    a. many   b. few   c. several

20. My neighborhood supermarket doesn't carry _____ exotic food products.

    a. all of   b. much of   c. a lot of

21. There are _____ smaller grocery stores near my house, too.

    a. a little   b. a couple   c. several

22. _____ the small stores stay open very late.

    a. All   b. Several   c. None

23. Since I have so _____ money, I avoid the small, expensive shops.

    a. much   b. little   c. few

24. There's a health food store around the corner, but it carries _____ foods that I really like.

    a. little   b. some   c. few

25. _____ children enjoy a trip to the supermarket more than their parents.

    a. Most   b. All of   c. More

UNIT 8 ANSWERS

A. **1.** a jar of (NC)   **2.** some (C)   **3.** a box of (C)   **4.** a head of (NC)   **5.** a jar of/a can of (NC)

B.   Some answers may vary.

6. eggs   **7.** cereal   **8.** jam, jelly, etc.   **9.** bread   **10.** butter

C. **11.** None of my friends likes lima beans.
   12. A few of these peaches are green.
   13. Most of my brothers and sisters are allergic to chocolate.
   14. They spend a lot of money at the supermarket.
   15. She speaks a little Greek.

D. **16.** c   **17.** b   **18.** c   **19.** b   **20.** c   **21.** c   **22.** a   **23.** b   **24.** c   **25.** a

Grammar Dimensions Book 2

Name _____

Unit 9 Degree Complements:
Too, Enough, and *Very*

Score _____
100

SECTION A
Complete the following using too or enough and any words in parentheses.

1. A: That waiter is always rude to me.

   B: Maybe you never leave a _____ tip. (big)

2. A: Aren't you going to finish your dessert?

   B: I can't. It's _____ . (rich). It must have a pound of butter in it.

3. A: I can hear everything the people at the next table are saying.

   B: So can I. The tables here are _____. (close together)

4. A: At least the portions are big. I've eaten _____ for three people!

5. B: Me too. But I don't think I'll come back. The service is _____ .(slow)

SECTION B
Re-write the following sentences using *too few* or *too little*.

6. We don't have enough eggs to make an omelette.

   _____.

7. There wasn't enough room in that apartment for a family of five.

   _____.

8. There aren't enough police on the streets.

   _____.

9. Not everyone can have a cookie. There aren't enough to go around.

   _____.

10. I haven't had enough time to get to the grocery store.

    _____.

SECTION C
Complete the following with *enough, not enough, too much/many/little/few, too + to* or *very* as appropriate.

I must admit I'm not a **(11)**_____ good traveler. First of all, I either pack

(12)_____ clothes and make my bag **(13)**_____ heavy

carry, or I take **(14)**_____ things and don't have **(15)**_____ to wear. I like to get to the airport (16)_____ early, but then I find I have (17) _____ time

to kill. I really hate flying. Everyone carries on (18)_____ luggage and there's never

(19)_____ room for it. I can't relax (20)_____ to sleep, there are

(21)_____ bathrooms for the number of passengers, and I always seem to sit next to

someone who talks (22)_____. The attendants have (23)_____time to

serve drinks, show a movie, and feed everyone, so they're usually (24)_____ busy

answer any questions. And the food is never (25)_____ appetizing, but at least it

helps pass the time.

UNIT 9 ANSWERS

A. 1. big enough 2. too rich 3. too close together 4. enough 5. too slow

B. 6. We have too few eggs to make an omelette.
   7. There was too little room in that apartment for a family of five.
   8. There are too few police on the street.
   9. There are too few cookies to go around.
   10. I've had too little time to get to the grocery store.

C. 11. very   12. too many   13. too..to   14. too few   15. enough   16. very
   17. too much   18. too much   19. enough   20. enough   21. too few
   22. too much   23. too little   24. too...to   25. very

Grammar Dimensions Book 2

Unit 10 Giving Advice and Expressing Opinions *Should, Ought To, Need To, Must, Had Better, Could,* and *Might*

Name _____

Score _____
100

SECTION A
Write sentences with *should, ought to,* and *shouldn't* that you might find in these self-help books.

Write three pieces of advice from *Healthy Cats, Happy Owners.*

   1. (feed)_____

   2. (play)_____

   3. (hit)_____

Write two pieces of advice from *Ten Steps to Better Grades.*

   4. (television)_____

   5. (before an exam)_____

SECTION B
Fill in the blanks with *should, shouldn't, must,* or *must not.* Sometimes more than one modal is possible.
Try to use each of them at least once.

   6. You _____ have a license to drive a car.

   7. You _____ keep your car clean and waxed.

   8. You _____ leave children or pets alone in your car.

   9. You _____ exceed the posted speed limit.

 10. You _____ pick up hitchhikers.

SECTION C
Complete these sentences with *should, ought to, need to,* or *shouldn't.* (Do not use *should* more than twice.)

11. Hurry up! Your train leaves in ten minutes. You _____ find a taxi now!

12. Nutritionists say you _____ eat five servings of fruits and vegetables a day.

13. You _____ go swimming after a big, heavy meal.

14. You _____ put some ice on your ankle; it's starting to swell.

15. I ought to exercise more often, and you _____, too.

SECTION D
Circle your choice in each of the following sentences.

16. In most cities you (shouldn't, must not) eat or drink when you ride the subway.

17. You (must, should) read the want-ads in the Sunday paper if you want to find a job.

18. It looks like someone broke down your front door. We (had better/should) call the police.

19. You (ought to/must) be 21 to enter the casino.

20. Carolyn (should/must) get out of the house more often. She studies too much.

21. You (had better/should) drive out into the country and enjoy the scenery.

22. Children under ten years old on this bus (must/should) be accompanied by an adult.

23. You (had better not/should not) miss any more of my lectures if you want to pass this course,

    Mr. Wilson.

24. You (should/must) get a library card. Books are so expensive!

25. They (should/had better) try that restaurant if they like Mexican food.

UNIT 10 ANSWERS

A. **1. - 5.** Students' own sentences

B. **6.** must **7.** should **8.** shouldn't **9.** mustn't **10.** shouldn't

C. **11.** need to **12.** should/ought to **13.** shouldn't **14.** should/ought to
15. should/ought to

D. **16.** must not **17.** should **18.** had better **19.** must **20.** should
21. should **22.** must **23.** had better not **24.** should **25.** should

Grammar Dimensions Book 2

Name _____

Unit 11 Modals of Necessity and Prohibition *HaveTo/Have Got To, Do Not Have To, Must/Must Not, Cannot*

Score _____
100

SECTION A
Circle your choice in each of the following sentences.

1. In public places, you (can/must) keep your dog on a leash.

2. You have a serious drug problem, Cindy. You (should/have got to) get some professional help.

3. See that sign? You (can/should) only park on the right side of this street.

4. You (have got to/should) pay your electricity bill as soon as it arrives.

5. You (cannot/should not) wash clothes in public fountains.

SECTION B
Use each of the following only once to complete the text: *can/have to/don't have to /must/must not*

Everyone knows that you **(6)**_____ be Italian to love pizza. If you want to make it at

home, you **(7)**_____ have a good but simple recipe for the crust. For best results, you

(8)_____ use only the freshest ingredients, and you **(9)**_____ reduce the

amount of cheese you use if you're worried about fat. If you really want to enjoy this American

favorite, you **(10)**_____ eat pizza with a knife and fork, only with your hands.

SECTION C
You and your friends have formed an English conversation club. Write some of its rules below, using the words in parentheses.

11. _____.

   (have to/an English name)

12. _____.

   (must/only English)

13. _____.

   (not have to/perfect English)

14. _____.

   (must not/dictionary)

15. _____.

   (have got to/five cents/foreign word)

SECTION D
Fill in the blanks in the text using the following: *can/cannot/have to/don't have to/must/must not/should*

Like all amusement parks, Disneyland was designed for people to have fun in. You can have a really good time if you follow some suggestions and obey certain regulations.

16. You _____ speak English to enjoy yourself in Disneyland.

17. You _____ wear comfortable, casual clothes.

18. You _____ bring small children into the park.

19. You _____ bring animals into the park.

20. You _____ enter the park without shoes.

21. You _____ remain fully dressed at all times.

22. You _____ buy or consume alcohol in Disneyland.

23. Sometimes you _____ wait in line for the more popular attractions.

24. You pay one price at the entrance; you _____ pay for individual rides.

25. For certain rides, you _____ meet a minimum height requirement.

UNIT 11 ANSWERS

A. 1. must 2. have got to 3. can 4. should 5. cannot

B. 6. don't have to 7. have to/must 8. must/have to 9. can 10. must not

C. Suggested sentences:
11. You have to use an English name at club meetings.
12. You must speak only English during meetings.
13. You don't have to speak perfect English.
14. You must not bring a dictionary to meetings.
15. Club members have got to pay five cents for every foreign word they use during meetings.

D. 16. don't have to 17. should 18. can 19. must not 20. must not 21. must 22. cannot
23. have to 24. don't have to 25. must

Grammar Dimensions Book 2

Unit 12 Expressing Likes and Dislikes

Name _____

Score _____
100

SECTION A

Complete these sentences with *either, neither, so,* and *too.*

1. I like spicy food and _____ does Nacib.

2. He doesn't smoke and _____ do I.

3. I can't drink coffee at night and he can't _____ .

4. He loves mint tea and I do _____ .

5. He never skips a meal and _____ do I.

SECTION B

Fill in the blanks with an auxiliary verb or the appropriate form of the verb to be to make the second statement agree with the first.

6. Rehana made a good score on her TOEFL. So _____ Olga.

7. Fatima and Ali won't be here tomorrow. Neither _____ we.

8. You haven't changed a bit! Neither _____ you.

9. The service was terrible. The food _____ too.

10. My mother has studied Spanish for years. So _____ mine.

SECTION C

Mitsuki needs a roommate. She's talking to Ada to see if they might be compatible. Write the women's responses to each other's underlined comments in the blanks.

Mitsuki: I'm asthmatic, so I can't stand any form of smoke—cigarettes, pipes, whatever.

Ada: **(11)**_____, so that won't be a problem.

Mitsuki: I'll have a glass of wine now and then, but I've never done drugs or given wild parties.

Ada: **(12)**_____ Gosh! We sound equally boring.

Mitsuki: Yes, don't we? Let's see... What else? I mostly listen to classical music and jazz. Do you like jazz?

Ada: Well, **(13)**_____ . I mean, I can take it or leave it. Actually, I watched a good documentary on Ella Fitzgerald last night.

Mitsuki: You did? **(14)**_____. Didn't you love her?

Ada: Still do, always will. Well, it's late. I should get going.

Mitsuki: **(15)**_____ I'll give you a call tomorrow.

SECTION D
Circle your choice in the following statements.

16. I (enjoy/like) to watch old movies.

17. (To sing/singing) in my college chorus is my favorite pasttime.

18. Martha has been to China and (Bruce has been/so has Bruce).

19. Her parents come from California but his (aren't/don't).

20. He studies at night but (she doesn't/so does she).

SECTION E
Put these short phrases in the correct order.

21. I/neither/do. _____

22. too/have/I _____

23. they/so/do _____

24. can't/either/he _____

25. so/mine/are _____

UNIT 12 ANSWERS

A. 1. so 2. neither 3. either 4. too 5. neither

B. 6. did 7. will 8. have 9. was 10. has

C. 11. Neither can I 12. Neither have I 13. Sort of/Kind of 14. So did I 15. So should I.

D. 16. like 17. Singing 18. so has Bruce 19. don't 20. she doesn't

E. 21. Neither do I. 22. I have too. 23. So do they. 24. He can't either. 25. So are mine.

Grammar Dimensions Book 2

Unit 13 Present Perfect with *Since* and *For*

SECTION A
Mr. Scott is interviewing Mei Chang for a job in his record store. Write the questions he asked her in order to get these responses:

1. _____?

Yes, I do. I work in a drugstore after school.

2. _____?

I started working there during my first year in high school.

3. _____?

I've worked there for two years now.

4. _____?

Yes, I do. I play the clarinet.

5. _____?

I've taken lessons since I was ten years old.

SECTION B
Write *For* or *Since* in the space before each time phrase.

6. _____ as long as I can remember

7. _____ the past few weeks

8. _____ the snowstorm

9. _____ he moved to Mexico

10. _____ most of her life

SECTION C
Indicate whether these sentences have the same or different meanings by circling S or D.

11. A. He has worked there two years.

 B. He has worked there for two years.   S   D

12. A. She played basketball for three years.

 B. She has played basketball for three years. S   D

13. A. She stopped working out for a long time.

 B. She hasn't worked out for a long time.   S   D

14. A. He has worn glasses for a long time.

    B. He started wearing glasses a long time ago.   S   D

15. (It's Friday. They got married on Satuday.)

    A. They've been married since Saturday.

    B. They've been married for almost a week.   S   D

SECTION D
Fill in the blanks with *since* or *for* or the appropriate form of the verb in parentheses.

I **(16)**_____ (know) Audrey for a couple of years. A few weeks ago I

(17)_____ (ask) her, "How long **(18)**_____(wear) your hair in a braid?"

"**(19)**_____ I was in college," she said. "I **(20)**_____ (not cut) it

(21)_____ at least five years." Last Saturday she **(22)**_____ (decide) to cut

her hair very short and **(23)**_____(go) straight to the hairdresser's. I

(24)_____ (not see) her **(25)**_____ she made the big decision.

UNIT 13 ANSWERS

A. **1.** Do you work?/Do you have a job now?   **2.** When did you start working there?
   3. How long have you worked there?   **4.** Do you play a musical instrument?
   5. How long have you taken lessons?

B. **6.** For **7.** For **8.** Since **9.** Since **10.** For

C. **11.** S **12.** D **13.** D **14.** S **15.** S

D. **16.** have known   **17.** asked   **18.** have you worn   **19.** Since   **20.** haven't cut
   21. for   **22.** decided   **23.** went   **24.** haven't seen   **25.** since

Grammar Dimensions Book 2

Name _____

Unit 14 Present Perfect and Simple Past
Ever and *Never*, *Already* and *Yet*

Score _____
100

SECTION A
Put the verb in parentheses in the simple past or the present perfect to complete the following sentences.

1. Anna's a good student. She _____(think) a lot about where she wants to study.

2. She _____(apply) to five colleges that are not too far from her hometown.

3. Last week she _____(receive) acceptance notices from three of them.

4. Some of Anna's friends _____(take) the college entrance exams more than once.

5. Mary and Wilton _____(take) them twice in their junior year and again last month.

SECTION B
Complete the conversations, using the present perfect or the simple past of the verb in parentheses. The first one has been done for you.

1. A. <u>Have you ever tasted</u> octopus salad before? (you/taste/ever)

    B. Octopus salad? Yes, I **(6)**_____ (taste) it. In fact I **(7)**_____ (eat) it

    lots of times.

    A. Where **(8)**_____ (you/try) it for the first time?

    B. I first **(9)**_____ (have) it in Portugal, in a little town called Sintra.

2. A. **(10)**_____ to England? (you/be/ever)

    B. As a matter of fact, I **(11)**_____ (be) there several times.

    A. When **(12)**_____ (go) there for the first time?

    B. About ten years ago, right after I **(13)**_____ (graduate) from college.

    A. **(14)**_____ (drive) when you were there?

    B. Are you kidding?! I **(15)**_____ on the left side of the road in my life, and I hope I

    never have to! (have/drive/never)

SECTION C
Put the letter of the right word or words in the space to complete the following.

16. Wake up! The alarm clock _____ twice.

   (a) went off already (b) has already gone off (c) has gone off yet

17. George _____ worked a day in his life.

   (a) has already (b) has never (c) has yet

18. _____ worked as a babysitter?

   (a) Have you ever (b) Did you already (c) Do you ever

19. She _____ nothing about her problem to me.

   (a) hasn't said (b) has never said (c) has said

20. Have you _____?

   (a) had dinner ever (b) had already dinner (c) had dinner yet

SECTION D
Write questions that correspond to the following answers.

21._____?

"T he Wizard of Oz"? Yes, I have. In fact, I've seen it dozens of times.

22. _____?

Oh, the first time I saw it was when I was about eight years old.

23. _____?

Today's newspaper? No, I haven't read it yet.

24. _____?

I'm afraid <u>I have</u> had lunch already. I couldn't wait for you.

25. _____?

No, Mom, I haven't taken the garbage out yet, but I'm just about to.

UNIT 14 ANSWERS

A. **1.** has thought **2.** has applied **3.** received **4.** have taken **5.** took

B. **6.** have tasted **7.** have eaten **8.** did you try **9.** had **10.** Have you ever been
11. have been **12.** did you go **13.** graduated **14.** Did you drive **15.** have never driven

C. **16.** b **17.** b **18.** a **19.** c **20.** c

D. **21.** Have you ever seen "The Wizard of Oz?"
22. When was the first time you saw it?/When did you first see it?
23. Have you read today's newspaper yet?
24. Have you already had lunch?
25. Have you taken out the garbage yet?

Grammar Dimensions Book 2

Name _____

Unit 15 Present Perfect Progressive

Score _____
100

SECTION A
Your cousin is visiting you for a week. When you get home in the evening you can see
how he's been spending his time. Write a sentence for each of your discoveries.

1. The TV is on. Your cousin is asleep on the sofa and the remote control is still in his hand.

_____.

2. Every pot and pan in the kitchen is dirty.

_____.

3. There was a lot of beer in the refrigerator last night. Now several cans are gone.

_____.

4. Your diary is open on your bed.

_____.

5. The ashtray on the coffee table is full and the living room smells of cigarette smoke.

_____.

SECTION B
Complete the following dialogues. The first one has been done for you.

a. Have you talked to your mother this week?

b. No, she <u>'s been spending</u> all her time with her new boyfriend. (spend)

6. Gas station attendant: Can I help you folks?

Andrew: I hope so. We _____ around for half an hour and we can't find this address. (drive)

7. Kate: Has your sister found a job yet?

Sam: No, but she _____ for very long. (not look)

8. John: Are Fran and Paula getting ready for their trip?

Paul: I guess so. They _____ a lot of maps and travel guides recently. (study)

9. Edith: I'm so tired I can't keep my eyes open.

Chris: _____ a lot at night? (cry/the baby)

10. Marian: I _____ in that flower bed since eight o'clock. (work)

Ed: Well, sit down and have some lemonade.

SECTION C
Read each situation and circle the letter of the statement that best describes it.

11. Terry started taking piano lessons when she was seven and stopped a few years later.

    a. Terry has been taking piano lessons.

    b. Terry has taken piano lessons since she was seven.

    c. Terry has taken piano lessons.

12. It's 6:30. Dinner is almost over and the children's hands and faces are all greasy.
    There are only two pieces of fried chicken left on the platter.

    a. They've eaten fried chicken.

    b. They've been eating fried chicken for a long time.

    c. They've been eating fried chicken.

13. Virginia knitted a sweater for me two years ago. She started knitting another one for me a
    month ago, but she's only finished the back. Her needles and the wool are on her chair now.

    a. Virginia has been knitting me sweaters for two years.

    b. Virginia has been knitting me a sweater.

    c. Virginia has knitted me two sweaters.

14. Bill made a short film when he was in college and he made another short film two years later.

    a. Bill's been making films for several years.

    b. Bill's been making films since college.

    c. Bill's made two films.

15. Rosemary went to France for two weeks last year. She also went in 1993 and 1995.

    a. She's been going to France since 1993.

    b. She's been to France three times.

    c. She's gone to France for two weeks.

SECTION D
Complete the dialogue using the present perfect progressive, the present perfect, or the simple past tense.

Allison: Where **(16)**_____ (you/be)? I **(17)**_____ (drive) around the block

for twenty minutes.

Tom: I **(18)**_____ (talk) to my math teacher. I **(19)**_____ (not do) all of the

homework assignments this term and I **(20)**_____ (fail) the last test, so...

Allison: But you **(21)**_____ (study) nothing but math for weeks.

Tom: I know, but I **(22)**_____ (not take) any math courses last year, so this one

(23)_____ (be) a lot harder. And the teacher **(24)**_____ (go) really fast

recently.

Allison: Well, let's get something to eat. I **(25)**_____(have/just) an apple, but I'm still

hungry.

UNIT 15 ANSWERS

A. **1.** He's been watching TV.   **2.** He's been cooking.   **3.** He's been drinking beer.
4. He's been reading my diary.   **5.** He's been smoking.

B. **6.** have been driving   **7.** hasn't been looking   **8.** have been studying
9. Has the baby been crying   **10.** have been working

C. **11.** c   **12.** c   **13.** b   **14.** c   **15.** b

D. **16.** have you been   **17.** have been driving   **18.** have been talking   **19.** haven't done
20. failed   **21.** have been studying   **22.** didn't take   **23.** has been
24. has been going   **25.** have just had

Grammar Dimensions Book 2

Name _____

Unit 16 Making Offers with *Would You Like*

Score _____
100

SECTION A

You've invited your future in-laws for dinner. It's the first time you've met them and they seem very formal. Change the following suggestions into polite offers using *Would you like.....?*

1. Another drink. _____

2. Wash your hands. _____

3. Let me get you some more bread. _____

4. Some more soup? _____

5. You don't look well. Let me call a doctor for you. _____

SECTION B

Write the letter of the appropriate response in the space before each offer.

6. Would you like Mark to help you?	a. Thank you, I'd love to.
7. Do you want another cup of coffee?	b. Not yet. He's in a bad mood.
8. Do you want me to tell Dad about the car?	c. Yes, please. They're delicious.
9. Would you like to see the garden?	d. Are you going to have one?
10. Would you like another brownie?	e. Thanks, but I can manage.

SECTION C

Write the letter of the correct phrase in the space.

11. My TV is broken. _____ some music?

    a. Would you like to listen   b. Would you like to hear   c. Do you want me

12. You look tired, honey. _____ to make you some coffee?

    a. Do you like me   b. Do you want   c. Would you like me

13. _____ and tell me all your troubles, son.

    a. Do you want to sit down   b. Sit down   c. Would you like to sit down

14. Excuse me. _____ a clean spoon, please?

    a. Do you want me to bring you   b. Would you bring me   c. Do you want to bring

15. Quiet down there! We're trying to sleep! _____ to call the police?

    a. Do you want   b. Would you like   c. Do you want us

SECTION D
You're in a clothing store. Complete the salesperson's remarks by filling in the blanks with an appropriate word or words.

Please come in. Let me know if I can help you with anything. Would you

(16)_____see a particular color? Would you like (17)_____ get you a

larger size? These have just come in. (18)_____ to try one on? The woman who does

our alterations is here today. Would you like (19)_____ make this shorter for you? Do

(20)_____ put that in a box or on a hanger for you?

SECTION E
Write offers that correspond to these responses.

21. _____.

Thanks very much, but I'll have to say no. I'm driving.

22. _____.

No, please don't get up. I'll close it.

23. _____.

Sure, why not? Are you going to have more, too?

24. _____.

Thank you. Ordinarily I'd love to stay, but I've already had dinner.

25. _____.

That's okay. I'll wash them. You did them last night.

A. 1. Would you like another drink?   2. Would you like to wash your hands?
3. Would you like me to get you some more bread?   4. Would you like some more soup?
5. Would you like me to call a doctor for you?

B. 6. e   7. d   8. b   9. a   10. c

C. 11. b   12. c   13. b   14. b   15. c

D. 16. like to   17. me to   18. Would you like   19. her to   20. you want me to

E. 21. Would you like another drink?   22. Do you want/Would you like me to close the window?   23. Would you like some more cake?   24. Would you like to stay for dinner?   25. Do you want/Would you like me to do the dishes/

Grammar Dimensions Book 2

Unit 17 Requests and Permission
Can/Could/Will/Would/May

Name _____

Score _____
100

SECTION A
Re-write the incorrect requests and make the others more polite by using the words provided.

1. Do you mind to give me a hand with these bags? (would)

_____.

2. Tell me when those books come in, okay? (will)

_____.

3. Hold that door for me! (could)

_____.

4. Please you turn down your radio. (would)

_____.

5. I've missed my bus, Dad. Drive me to school. (can)

_____.

SECTION B
Write a polite request for each situation using one of the following: *will, can, mind, may, could*

6. The people behind you at the movie keep talking. You finally turn around and say politely:

_____?

7. You ask someone for directions to the library. He speaks so fast that you don't understand the

directions at all. You say:

_____?

8. You're holding a baby, a shopping bag, and the Sunday paper. Your hands are full and you

need to use the phone. Ask your friend for help:

_____?

9. You're at the dinner table. You can't reach the salt, but you think your sister can. Ask her to pass

it to you.

_____?

10. A friendly-looking stranger is walking a tiny new puppy in the park. You don't want to touch the dog without the owner's permission, so you say:

_____?

SECTION C
Write the letter of the appropriate response in the space by each number.

11. Could you lend me fifty dollars?   **a.** Sure. Just a second.

My electricity bill is due._____

12. Would you mind very much driving me   **b.** I could, but why don't you just come with me?

to the post office?_____

13. Will you see who's at the door?_____   **c.** Are you asking or telling me to?

14. Make sure you water my plants   **d.** Not at all. I'd be happy to.

while I'm gone.

15. You're going to the store? Can you   **e.** Sorry. I'd like to help you, but I can't.

pick up some ice cream?_____

SECTION D
Fill in the blanks with the missing word or words.

A. Dad, **(16)**_____ the car tonight? I'm going over to Stephanie's to study.

B. Sorry, I'm **(17)**_____I need it. Why don't you ask her to come here for dinner?

A. **(18)**_____ I? Thanks. **(19)**make us one of your incredible pizzas?

B. **(20)**_____ . **(21)**_____ running out to the store for some olive oil?

A. **(22)**_____ glad to. Now **(23)**_____ the keys to the car?

B. Of course, but **(24)**_____ taking your brothers with you?

A. Not **(25)**_____.

UNIT 17 ANSWERS

A.
1. Would you mind giving me a hand with these bags?
2. Will you tell me when those books come in (please)?
3. Could you (please) hold that door for me?
4. Would you (please) turn down your radio?
5. Can you (please) drive me to school?
6. Would you mind not talking?
7. Could you speak more slowly (please)?
8. Will you hold the baby for me (please)?
9. Can you pass me the salt (please)?
10. May I pet your dog?

B. 11. e 12. d 13. a 14. c 15. b

C. 16. Can/could I borrow/use   17. afraid   18. Can   19. Will/Would you   20. Sure./Certainly.

D. 21. Would you mind   22. I'd be   23. may I have   24. would you mind   25. at all

Grammar Dimensions Book 2

Name _____

Unit 18 *Used to* with *Still* and *Anymore*

Score _____
100

SECTION A
Put the verbs in parentheses in the correct form (the simple past, the present tense, *used to,* or *didn't use to*).

Ten years ago, Philip and Ann **(1)**_____ (move) to the country because they

(2)_____ (want) to write a book. They **(3)**_____ (give) away their TV and

Philip **(4)** _____ (stop) shaving. Last year they **(5)**_____ (rent) a house in a

big city and **(6)**_____ (get) nine-to-five jobs in offices. They always

(7)_____ (sleep) late in the country, but these days they **(8)**_____ (get up)

at seven o'clock. Philip **(9)**_____ (shave) every morning now, but he

(10)_____ (not shave) in the country.

SECTION B
Write sentences about Philip and Ann's life in the country using *used to* and *didn't use to* with the words provided.

11. (grow their own vegetables) _____.

12. (watch TV)_____.

13. (wear jeans everyday)_____.

14. (Philip/a beard)_____.

15. (get up early)_____.

SECTION C
Complete the following with *still* or *anymore.*

16. They love fresh bread, but they don't bake their own _____.

17. Turn that music down! People are _____ sleeping.

18. Is there someone else? Don't you love me _____?

19. Some people _____ don't believe that man has walked on the moon.

20. I love my computer; I hardly ever use my typewriter _____ .

SECTION D
Circle the letter that indicates where the frequency adverb should be placed in each sentence.

21. She (a) used (b) to (c) smoke cigars, but she does (d) now. (never)

22. (a) We (b) have (c) any news from our cousins (d) in Canada. (seldom)

23.(a) Mike and Steve (b) don't (c) go (d) to the movies on weeknights. (usually)

24. He (a) has (b) wanted (c) to (d) go back to school. (always)

25. (a) He (b) was (c) sick (d) as a child. (often)

UNIT 18 ANSWERS

A.   **1.** moved   **2.** wanted   **3.** gave   **4.** stopped   **5.** rented   **6.** got
   7. used to   **8.** get up   **9.** shaves   **10.** didn't use to

B.   **11.** They used to grow their own vegetables.   **12.** They didn't use to watch TV.
   13. They used to wear jeans every day.   **14.** Philip used to have a beard.
   15. They didn't use to get up early.

C.   **16.** anymore   **17.** still   **18.** anymore   **19.** still   **20.** anymore

D.   **21.** a   **22.** b   **23.** c   **24.** b   **25.** c

Grammar Dimensions Book 2

Unit 19 Past Perfect *Before* and *After*

Name _____

Score _____
100

SECTION A
Put the verbs in parentheses in the simple past or past perfect tense.

1. By the time Mozart _____ (be) eight years old, he _____ (compose) a

lot of music.

2. When I _____ (get) home the next day, I could see that my roommates

_____ (have) a party.

3. The exam _____ (already + begin) by the time I _____ (find) the right

classroom.

4. We _____ (just + sit) down at the dinner table when the doorbell

_____ (ring).

5. When your grandparents _____ (be) children, television _____ (not

be) invented.

SECTION B
Join the two sentences to make one sentence, using *because* or *by the time*.

6. The ice cream melted. We got home from the supermarket.

_____.

7. Her car ran out of gas. She asked to use our telephone.

_____.

8. The rain stopped. We arrived at the station.

_____.

9. Bill was angry. His computer crashed.

_____.

10. Karen couldn't walk. She broke her ankle.

_____.

SECTION C
There is a mistake in each of the following sentences. Circle it and write your correction in the space provided. Use the simple past or past perfect tense.

11. Kevin is happy because his favorite soccer team had won the game _____.

12. Mark was upset because Kate has forgotten his birthday._____.

13. Lisa and Gabriel have lived in Texas for years, but they have never been to Mexico until last

week.. _____.

14. Margie doesn't want to go out for pizza because she had had it for dinner last night.

_____.

15. Susan and Russell are tired because they had worked twelve hours that day.

_____.

SECTION D
Put the verb in parentheses in the appropriate tense. Use the simple past, the past
progressive, the present perfect, or the past perfect tense.

Nita and Paul **(16)**_____ (be) engaged for three years now. They first

(17)_____ (meet) when they **(18)**_____ (study) English at the community

college. By the time the course **(19)**_____ (end) they **(20)**_____ (decide) to

get married. A few months ago, Paul's company **(21)**_____(transfer) him to San Fran-

cisco. Nita **(22)**_____(go) to visit him last week, and since she **(23)**

(be/never) to California before, it was a really exciting trip. She **(24)**_____ (get back)

on Sunday and is full of their wedding plans. Her friends **(25)**_____ (see/never) her

look happier than she does these days.

UNIT 19 ANSWERS

A. **1.** was; had composed   **2.** got; had had   **3.** had already begun; found
     4. had just sat; rang   **5.** were; hadn't been

B. **6.** By the time we got home from the supermarket, the ice cream had melted.
     7. She asked to use our telephone because her car had run out of gas.
     8. By the time we arrived at the station, the rain had stopped.
     9. Bill was angry because his computer had crashed.
    10. Karen couldn't walk because she had broken her ankle.

C. **11.** Kevin <u>was</u> happy...   **12.** ...<u>had</u> forgotten   **13.** they <u>had</u> never been
    14. she <u>had</u> it for dinner   **15.** <u>were</u> tired

D. **16.** have been   **17.** met   **18.** were studying   **19.** ended   **20.** had decided
    21. transferred   **22.** went   **23.** had never been   **24.** got back   **25.** have never seen

Grammar Dimensions Book 2

Name _____

Unit 20 Articles

Score _____
100

SECTION A
Fill in the blanks with *a/an/some/the/* or ∅.

1. When I was _____ child, my family used to spend _____ week every summer in Maine.

2. _____ friends of my parents had a cabin there, and they would give us _____ keys.

3. The cabin was on _____ lake, at the top of a steep hill that was covered in _____ pine trees.

4. There was _____ large fireplace in _____ living room of the cabin and the living room was two stories high.

5. Needless to say, the cabin almost never got warm, and _____ mornings we would stand in front of the fireplace and pull on _____ jeans and sweaters as quickly as we could.

6. The cabin had no bathroom, but there was _____ outhouse which seemed to a child (but wasn't) very far from the cabin, hidden among _____ trees.

7. I remember having wonderful breakfasts of _____ pancakes made on _____ pot-bellied stove in the kitchen.

8. I had never seen _____ pot-bellied stove anywhere else, and I was fascinated. My mother would get _____ wood from outside and let me put it in the stove.

9. When the sun had warmed _____ hillside a bit, we would climb slowly down the hill in our bathing suits to go swimming in _____ icy lake.

10. The cabin in Maine wasn't _____ especially comfortable place, but I spent _____ of the happiest days of my life there.

SECTION B
Fill in the blanks with *the* or ∅.

11. Your plants are all dying. They need _____ sun.

12. This jacket is made of wool, but _____ lining is made of silk.

13. Money can't buy _____ happiness.

14. Home is where _____ heart is.

15. The road to hell is paved with _____ good intentions.

SECTION C
Find the mistake in each sentence and correct it. Use the space provided if necessary.

16. Americans drink gallons of the coffee every day. _____.

17. I bought some interesting book. _____.

18. Sam listens to radio all day, every day. _____.

19. He has a old used car that needs painting. _____.

20. Children in that family are very bright. _____.

SECTION D
Write your answers to the following questions in complete sentences.

21. What kind of winter coat do you need?

_____.

22. Which restaurant in this area do you like best?

_____.

23. If you flew to another city and the airline lost your luggage, what would you need to buy?

_____.

24. What did you eat and drink between five p.m. and midnight yesterday?

_____.

25. What do you want for your birthday?

_____.

UNIT 20 ANSWERS

Each answer in numbers 1-10 counts two points.

A. **1.** a; a   **2.** Some/∅; the   **3.** a; ∅   **4.** a; the   **5.** some; ∅
   6. an; the   **7.** ∅; the   **8.** a; some/∅   **9.** the; the   **10.** an; some

B. **11.** ∅ **12.** the **13.** ∅ **14.** the **15.** ∅

C. **16.** ...gallons of (∅) coffee   **17.** ... <u>an</u> interesting/...interesting <u>books</u>   **18.** ... <u>the</u> radio
   19. ...<u>an</u> old   **20.** <u>The</u> children...

D. **21. - 25.** Students' own sentences.

Grammar Dimensions Book 2

Unit 21 Articles with Names of Places

Name _____

Score _____

100

SECTION A
Fill in the blanks with *the* or ∅.

The historic and commercial center of Philadelphia is located between

(1)_____ Delaware and Schuylkill Rivers. A statue of its founder, William Penn,

watches over the city from the top of **(2)**_____ City Hall. Once the capital of

(3)_____ United States, Philadelphia is visited year round by tourists who line up to

see such attractions as **(4)**_____ Liberty Bell in **(5)**_____ Independence

National Park and the home of Betsy Ross, the woman credited with sewing the first American

flag. The city is also home to a number of educational and cultural institutions including

(6)_____ University of Pennsylvania, **(7)**_____ Temple University, and

(8)_____ Philadelphia Museum of Art. On weekends, students from

(9)_____ Penn, as the locals call the university, head for the clubs and restaurants of

(10)_____ South Street, the heart of the city's nightlife.

SECTION B
Write a sentence about each of the following (the first one has been done for you):

(a city you would like to visit)

I'd like to see Paris from the top of the Eiffel Tower.

11. (a school or institute you have attended)

_____.

12. (a river near where you live)

_____.

13. (a country you would like to visit)

_____.

14. (a museum you have visited)

_____.

15. (a monument you have seen or would like to see)

_____.

SECTION C
Write *the* or ∅ in the spaces.

16. When most people think of New York, they think of _____ island of Manhattan.

17. Did you know that millions of New Yorkers have never visited _____ Statue of

    Liberty?

18. Is _____ Martha's Vineyard an island?

19. Of course. And so is _____ Nantucket.

20. People in _____ South have a reputation for being very friendly.

21. He learned to swim in _____ Lake Michigan, but he said he's never liked it much.

22. Imagine how easy it must be to swim in _____ Red Sea, with all that salt to hold

    you up.

23. I'd love to ride on an old steamboat down _____ Mississippi River.

24. I'd rather cross the U.S. by car and drive from New York to Los Angeles

    on _____ Route 66.

25. Naturally, I'd stop at _____ Grand Canyon on the way.

UNIT 21 ANSWERS

A. 1. the 2. ∅ 3. the 4. the 5. ∅ 6. the 7. ∅ 8. the 9. ∅ 10. ∅

B. 11. - 15. Students' own sentences.

C. 16. the 17. the 18. ∅ 19. ∅ 20. the 21. ∅ 22. the 23. the 24. ∅ 25. the

Grammar Dimensions Book 2

Name _____

Unit 22 The Passive

Score _____
100

SECTION A
Match each situation with one of the previous events.

1. _____ That's not what your mother told me, young man.

2. _____ Please clean out your desk and turn in your key to the office.

3. _____ Quick! Grab the food and bring it inside!

4. _____ I'd like to call my lawyer.

5. _____ I didn't know it had just come out of the oven.

6. _____ Great, but now I'll have to rent a tuxedo.

7. _____ You mean, the land we bought is worthless?

8. _____ Sorry we're late. You know how rush hour is.

a. She got burned.   e. They got held up in traffic.

b. He got caught in a lie.   f. He got invited to a black-tie dinner.

c. They got ripped off.   b. The picnic got rained out.

d. She got fired.   h. He got arrested.

SECTION B
Complete the following in the passive voice, using the appropriate tenses.

No one knows exactly how many movies **(9)**_____ (make) in the United States since

the art form was invented. Many of the first films **(10)**_____ (shoot) in and around

New York City, but the industry soon moved west. By the 1920's, Hollywood, an undistinguished

tract of land in Southern California, **(11)**_____ (transform) into what

(12)_____ (call, sometimes) the Dream Factory. In the early years, movies

(13)_____ (produce) in a matter of days or weeks by relatively small crews, and elab-

orate sets **(14)**_____ (build) on huge sound stages to represent exotic places. Modern

movies, of course, take much longer to make. Hundreds of people may

(15)_____ (involve) in their production, and most movies **(16)**_____ (film)

on location. Up until perhaps the end of the 1950's, movie studios had tremendous power over

the stars they created. Actors **(17)**_____ (tell) exactly what films they would make, and many facets of their personal lives **(18)**_____ (arrange) for them. But the so-called

star system died out, and the whole industry **(19)**_____ (change) by the advent of

television. Going to the pictures is no longer considered an exciting event but, thanks to the video

cassette recorder, more movies **(20)**_____ (see) than ever before.

SECTION C
Re-write the following statements in the passive voice.

21. Archaeologists have recently discovered mummies in Peru.

_____.

22. The Incas buried them about 500 years ago.

_____.

23. The mechanic is repairing my car today.

_____.

24. They will hold the meeting in the school auditorium at 8 o'clock on Tuesday.

_____.

25. A ten-year-old Romanian girl did all of these oil paintings.

_____.

UNIT 22 ANSWERS

A. 1. b   2. d   3. g   4. h   5. a   6. f   7. c   8. e

B. 9. have been made   10. were shot   11. had been transformed   12. is sometimes called
13. were produced   14. were built   15. be involved   16. are filmed   17. were told
18. were arranged   19. was changed   20. are seen

C. 21. Mummies have been discoved in Peru.
22. They were buried by the Incas about 500 years ago.
23. My car is being repaired today.
24. The meeting will be held in the school auditorium at 8 o'clock on Tuesday.
25. All of these oil paintings were done by a ten-year-old Romanian girl.

Grammar Dimensions Book 2

Unit 23 Phrasal Verbs

Name _____

Score _____
100

SECTION A
Fill in the blanks with the correct particle. Use *back, down, out,* or *to.*

1. As soon as you come _____ from the store, we can start making dinner.

2. When Joan's father passed _____ on the sidewalk, she thought he was dead.

3. After he came _____ in the hospital, the doctor told him he needed surgery.

4. She was offered a small role in a movie, but she turned it _____ .

5. The pen I just bought doesn't write, so I'll have to take it _____ to the store.

SECTION B
Replace the underlined words in each sentence with a phrasal verb.

6. They <u>postponed</u> the party because of the snowstorm. _____.

7. He <u>distributed</u> the tests and told us to begin. _____.

8. Has your car ever <u>stopped working</u> in the middle of the freeway? _____.

9. He has to <u>collect</u> his children after school. _____.

10. Let's <u>telephone</u> Angela and Hugo and see if they want to go out for pizza._____.

11. They never <u>go to restaurants</u> now because they're saving for a trip. _____.

12. How did she <u>discover</u> that we were planning a surprise party for her? _____.

13. I <u>encountered</u> an old friend on my way to work today. _____.

14. Please <u>remove</u> your coat and stay a while. _____.

15. When you <u>board</u> the bus, ask the driver if he stops at 16th Street. _____.

SECTION C
Use a phrasal verb in an appropriate statement, suggestion, or polite request for each of the following:

16. A friend asks you what a certain word means. You're not sure yourself and there's a dictionary at hand, so you say: _____.

17. Your uncle's garage is filled with stacks of old newspapers. He says he has no use for them, so you ask: _____.

18. You need to leave the house for about 20 minutes. You don't want to take your child, who has a bad cold, but you can't leave him alone, either. Your neighbor drops in for a cup of coffee, so you ask: _____.

19. Your brother is leaving the house to meet some friends for dinner at an elegant restaurant.

He's wearing shorts and a T-shirt, so you say: _____.

20. You're watching a cooking program on TV. The dish the chef is making looks delicious. You

know you'll never remember the recipe, so you grab a pen and paper and say:

_____.

SECTION D
In the following sentences, cross out the word that is in the wrong place and indicate its correct position in the sentence. Then substitute a pronoun for the object and write the verb + object phrase in the space.

Example: She pointed a big mistake in the third paragraph out. _____.

21. He put his shoes, clothes, books, and all his sports equipment away.

_____.

22. You should start studying for exams now. If you put studying until the last minute off, you

won't do well. _____.

23. How can you buy shoes from a catalogue? Don't you want to try the shoes first on?

_____.

24. He didn't understand the homework, so we went again over the homework.

_____.

25. Margie wants to talk her plans with a good lawyer over.

_____.

UNIT 23 ANSWERS

A. **1.** back..**2.** out..**3.** to..**4.** down..**5.** back

B. **6.** put off   **7.** handed out   **8.** broken down   **9.** pick up   **10.** call up
11. eat out   **12.** find out   **13.** ran into   **14.** take off   **15.** get on

C. **16.** Let's look it up.
17. Why don't you throw them out?
18. Could you look after the baby for half an hour?
19. Why don't you put on a jacket and tie?
20. I'd better write this down.

D. **21.** He put away his shoes.../He put them away.
22. If you put off studying .../If you put it off...
23. Don't you want to try on the shoes first?/try them on
24. ...so we went over the homework again./went over it again
25. Margie wants to talk over her plans with a good lawyer./talk them over

Grammar Dimensions Book 2

Unit 24 Adjective Clauses

Name _____

Score _____
100

SECTION A
Combine each pair of sentences using adjective clauses.

1. A boy lives next door to me. He studies physics.

_____.

2. Some students speak Italian. They love to watch Fellini movies.

_____.

3. I don't like some people. They ask to copy my homework.

_____.

4. The teacher helps some students. They've worked hard.

_____.

5. Some students didn't study. They failed the exam.

_____.

SECTION B
Put the words in the correct order to make sentences.

6. man/television/Apartment 4C/the/in/who/all/day/watches/lives

_____.

7. I/just/Christmas/for/read/me/the/gave/book/that/you

_____.

8. call/cousins/in/live/never/New Jersey/our/us/who

_____.

9. the/which/all/illegible/notes/are/lent/he/me

_____.

10. downstairs/supermarket/woman/saw/lives/he/the/who/at/the

_____.

SECTION C
Complete the following to make true statements. Choose the appropriate relative pronoun.

11. I don't eat _____ (that/which/who) _____.

12. _____ (that/which/who) _____ are crazy.

13. I like _____ (that/which/who) _____.

14. _____ (that/which/who) _____ is very expensive.

15. This school needs _____ (that/which/who) _____.

SECTION D
Choose the correct adjectives in the following sentences.

16. I asked George if he wanted to go on the picnic with us, but he just said he was busy. I don't think he found the plan particularly (exciting/excited).

17. I also invited Brian, who's traveled all over the world and has such great stories to tell. He's a much more (interesting/interested) person than George.

18. I was (fascinating/fascinated) by Brian's account of his trip to Turkey.

19. He seemed very (disappointing/disappointed) that he didn't have more time to spend there.

20. I don't think the American consulate was very (amused/amusing) by Brian's losing his passport.

21. They must find all those tourists with their little problems very (annoying/annoyed).

22. Brian said his flight was cheap. I was (tempting/tempted) to ask how much it cost, but I didn't.

23. He and I both love London. The last time I was there I was really (mystifying/mystified) by a language I heard some people speaking. It turned out to be English, and the speakers were from my hometown.

24. Brian and I agreed that prices in London are really (shocking/shocked).

25. We were (relieving/relieved) to get back home before our money ran out.

UNIT 24 ANSWERS

A. 1. The boy who lives next door to me studies physics.
    2. The students who speak Italian love to watch Fellini movies.
    3. I don't like people who ask to copy my homework.
    4. The teacher helps students who have worked hard.
    5. The students who didn't study failed the exam.

B. 6. The man who lives in Apartment 4C watches television all day.
    7. I just read the book that you gave me for Christmas.
    8. Our cousins who live in New Jersey never call us.
    9. All the notes which he lent me are illegible.
   10. He saw the woman who lives downstairs at the supermarket.

C. 11. - 15. Students' own sentences.

D. 16. exciting   17. interesting   18. fascinated   19. disappointed   20. amused
   21. annoying   22. tempted   23. mystified   24. shocking   25. relieved

Grammar Dimensions Book 2

Name _____

Unit 25 Conditionals

Score _____
100

SECTION A
Write the letter of the possible result in the space next to the appropriate *if* clause.

1. _____ If I don't take my umbrella,   **a.)** I won't graduate.

2. _____ If I get wet,   **b.)** I won't make good grades.

3. _____ If I'm in bed for a week,   **c.)** it will probably rain.

4. _____ If I get behind in my studies,   **d.)** my parents will be really upset.

5. _____ If I do really badly,   **e.)** I may catch cold.

6. _____ If I have to repeat this year,   **f.)** I'll miss school.

SECTION B
Answer the questions in complete sentences.

7. If a fire broke out in your house, what would you do first?

_____.

8. If you had time, what personal possessions would you try to save from the fire?

_____.

9. If you were confined to your house, what would you do?

_____.

10. If you could talk to anyone in history, who would it be?

_____.

11. If you could have any job you wanted (and the skills to do it), what would you choose?

_____.

SECTION C
Fill in the blank with the correct form of the verb in parentheses.

12. A: I just heard that you were in the hospital for a month. If I _____ (know) you

were sick, I _____ (visit) you. What was wrong?

   B: I lost control of my bike on a curve and fell down a hill. Luckily, I had on a helmet.

13. A: Wow. I wonder what _____ (happen) if you _____ (not have on) a

helmet. How was your stay in the hospital?

14. B: Let's just say that if I never _____ (eat) hospital food again for the rest of my

life, I _____ (be) very happy.

15. A: You poor thing! If my refrigerator _____ (not be) empty at the moment, I

_____ (invite) you over for dinner tonight. How about this weekend?

16. If you _____ (tell) me what you'd like, I _____ (cook) it for you on Sat-

urday.

17. A: Maria is so lucky. Her mother is Cuban and her father is from Beijing. When she

_____ (finish) her degree, she _____ (be able) to teach three languages:

English, Spanish, and Chinese.

18. B: If I _____ (speak) all those languages, I _____ (want) to work as an

interpreter.

19. A: When you _____ (get) to the top of the hill, you _____ (see) a small

church. Walk past it and turn left, and the hotel is right there.

20. B: Thanks. I _____ (be) back for more help if I _____ (not find) it.

   A: You'll find it.

SECTION D
Complete these conversations with *will, would, may, might, would have, might have,* or
may have and the correct form of the verb in parentheses.

21. A: If I take that job, I _____ (need) to buy a car, I don't know.

22. B: Well, I hope not. You don't know how to take care of one. Remember the last car you had? If

you'd had an accident in that , you _____ (be) killed.

23. A. Oh, probably not. If I decide to get a car, _____ (help/you) me pick it out?

24. A. If I'd known you were coming, I _____ (go) to the station to meet you.

25. B. I'm glad you didn't. There were so many people that I _____ (not see) you.

UNIT 25 ANSWERS

A. **1.** c **2.** e **3.** f **4.** b **5.** a **6.** d

B. **7. - 11.** Students' own sentences.

C. **12.** had known, would have visited   **13.** would have happened, hadn't had on
14. eat, will be   **15.** weren't, would invite   **16.** tell, will cook   **17.** finishes, will be able
18. spoke, would want   **19.** get, will see   **20.** will be, don't find

D. **21.** may need   **22.** would have been   **23.** will you help
24. would have gone   **25.** might not have seen

Unit 1

Simple Present Habits, Routines, and Facts

EXERCISE 1

work; like; study; listen; raise; have; try; helps; rewrite; ask; helps

doesn't participate; interrupts; whispers; eats; drinks; pays attention; does

EXERCISE 2

Sentences will vary.
1. A good student works hard to improve his/her writing.   **2.** He/she studies hard.   **3.** She/he listens carefully to the directions.   **4.** He/she raises his/her hand when he/she has a question.   **5.** She/he tries to encourage other students.   **6.** A bad student doesn't participate in class.   **7.** He/she interrupts the teacher.   **8.** She/he whispers to other students.   **9.** He/she never pays attention.   **10.** She/he hardly ever does her/his assignments.

EXERCISE 3

2. Suzette and Raul write...   **3.** Yaniv and Valentina don't read...   **4.** Yaniv doesn't...   **5.** Yaniv doesn't watch...   **6.** Jean-Marc and Wan-Yin speak...   **7.** Su-

Ling goes...   **8.** Roberto practices...   **9.** Mohammed watches...   **10.** Wan-Yin doesn't...

EXERCISE 4

Add "Do you..." to make questions with the ideas from Exercise **3.** Answers will be "Yes, I do./No, I don't." Record of answers: "Yes, He/she does./No, He/she doesn't.

EXERCISE 5

1. has   **2.** changes   **3.** lives   **4.** swims   **5.** eats
6. builds   **7.** flies   **8.** washes   **9.** catches
10. breathes   **11.** sits

EXERCISE 6

Answers will vary.

EXERCISE 7

Answers will vary.
1. I sometimes...   **2.** I never...   **3.** I always...
4. I hardly ever...   **5.** I usually...   **6.** I seldom...
7. I rarely...   **8.** I often...   **9.** I sometimes...
10. I usually...

isn't smiling; today; isn't eating; 's
ho...

now; 's fasting; this month; isn't eating, drinking, smoking; 's trying

EXERCISE 2

1. Is; typing; is   2. is using/'s using; is   3. are you filing; 'm not/am not; is   4. is dying/'s dying; am/'m watering   5. Are you checking; are you checking; am/'m checking   6. are they standing; are/'re punching   7. are they filling   8. are you wearing; 'm wearing   9. is/'s he taking   10. is/'s he quitting

EXERCISE 3

(1) is running	(2) competes	(3) has
(4) is training	(5) swims	(6) runs
(7) is swimming	(8) is running	(9) works
(10) is lifting	(11) is bicycling	(12) is
(13) eats	(14) is making	(15) eats/is eating
(16) is trying	(17) is	(18) is

EXERCISE 4

This exercise really encourages the students to listen if all of their photographs are similar in theme (e.g., tell them to bring a picture of two women/men/children, two people on the telephone, or two people playing a sport).

EXERCISE 5

(1) is	(2) are	(3) travel
(4) are staying	(5) have	(6) think
(7) is	(8) don't own	(9) are taking
(10) isn't/is not	(11) is	(12) is
(13) tries	(14) thinks	
(15) doesn't understand		(16) knows
(17) are trying	(18) are treating	
(19) take	(20) play	(21) doesn't know
(22) is training	(23) is learning	(24) is beginning
(25) are looking	(26) love	(27) seems
(28) belongs	(29) loves	

EXERCISE 6

S = State Quality/Possession   A = Action/Experience
1. S   2. S   3. A   4. S   5. A   6. S   7. A   8. S   9. A   10. A
11. S   12. S   13. A   14. S   15. A

EXERCISE 7

ACROSS:
2. ensemble   8. opera   10. or   12. baaa   13. be
14. GE   15. SOS   16. echo   19. tete   20. torn
21. beta   22. HRS   23. nor   24. ED   25. cana
29. MC   30. finito   32. teachers

DOWN:
1. together   3. SOB   4. EPA   5. mea   6. bra
7. la   9. research   11. record   13. bottom   15. seen
17. HRS   18. on   19. TB   25. CIA   26. ANC
27. NIH   28. ate   30. fe   31. or

Unit 3

Talking About the Future *Be Going to* and *Will*

EXERCISE 1

Nancy's mother: We're going to go shopping this weekend; you'll look
Nancy: I'm not going to spend; I'll wear
Nancy's mother: will pay
Nancy: I'm going to wear
Tim: I'm going to wear
Nancy's mother: We're going to have
Nancy: Will have
Nancy's mother: it'll be; I'll ask; tonight

EXERCISE 2

Questions and answers will vary.

EXERCISE 3

(1) will   (2) will   (3) won't/will not   (4) will
(5) will   (6) won't/will not   (7) will   (8) won't/will
not   (9) 'm going to/am going to   (10) 'm going
to/am going to   (11) 'm going to/am going to
(12) 'm going to/am going to   (13) 'm going to/am
going to/will   (14) will/are going to   (15) are going
to/'re going to   (16) 'm going to/am going to

EXERCISE 4

Answers will vary.

EXERCISE 5

1. I'll get it right away.   2. I'll be on time from now
on./It won't happen again.   3. I'm going to go in July.
4. I'll help you.   5. I'll call her as soon as I can.   6. I
won't tell anyone.   7. It'll be better next year.   8. It
won't happen again.

EXERCISE 6

ACROSS:
1. fortune   6. Al   7. ok   9. AC   11. do   13. in
14. oh   15. saw   17. pie   18. spend   19. shelf
20. never   24. sweet   27. dad   28. ICU   29. rr
30. tu   31. ad   33. or   34. men   35. mom
37. sadness

DOWN:
1. fa   2. old   3. non   4. EK   5. Cassandra   8. the
future   10. cap   12. odd   13. its   14. oil   16. we
17. PE   21. ear   22. VD   23. round   24. Shame
25. EI   26. eco   30. tea   32. dos   34. MS   36. Ms.

TOEFL Exercises

Units 1-3 Answer Key

1.B	4. C	7. B	10. D	13. D	16. B	19. D	22. D	25. A	28. A
2. B	5. B	8. C	11. A	14. A	17. B	20. C	23. A or B	26. A	29. C
3. A	6. A	9. B	12. C	15. B	18. A	21.C	24. A	27. C	30. B

Unit 4

Asking Questions *Yes/No, Wh-,* Tag Questions

EXERCISE 1

2. Do; study   3. Is; living   4. Will; study   5. Would; eat   6. Is   7. Are; working   8. Am   9. Were; working   10. Was   11. Did; take   12. Do; sing

EXERCISE 2

Questions and answers will vary.

EXERCISE 3

1. You can swim?   2. You usually study on Saturday?
3. Your mother is living in the United States right now?
4. You'll study English next year?   5. You would eat red meat?   6. English is a difficult language for you?
7. You're working right now?   8. I'm taller than you?
9. You were working last night?   10. Mathematics was your favorite subject in elementary school?   11. You took a vacation last summer?   12. You sometimes sing in the shower?

EXERCISE 4

Questions will vary.

EXERCISE 5

Questions may vary.
What do you think your strong points are?   Are you looking for a full-time or part-time position?   What is your native country?/Where are you from?   When did you leave your last job?   Why did you leave it?
What kind of computers do you know how to use?
When will you be available to work?   How do you get to work?   When can you start working?   How much do you expect to earn?

EXERCISE 6

Questions will vary.

EXERCISE 7

2. Who is the oldest? Ken...   3. Who played basketball in high school? Ken...   4. Who visited Korea last vacation? Joy...   5. Who will start college next year? Bill is entering...   6. Who is the youngest? Bill...   7. Who likes Chinese food? Joy...   8. Who has children? Ken...
9. Who likes sports? Ken...

10. Who is the middle child? Joy...   11. Who is married? Ken...   12. Who is single? Joy and Bill are...   13. Who is a pilot? Ken...   14. Who is artistic? Bill...   15. Who sings? Bill...

EXERCISE 8

1. Who climbed the mountains to study the birds in the past?   2. What did bird watchers climb in the past to...
3. Who can watch the vultures from a museum in the village of Aste-Beon, France?   4. What can visitors do from...   5. What recorded the birds?   6. What did the television cameras record?   7. Who watched the birds on TV monitors?   8. What did visitors watch...
9. What can they do?   10. Whom can they see fly and feed?   11. What can visitors see the birds do?
12. What can visitors see the birds hatch?   13. What will you do in Aste-Beon next year?   14. What will you visit in...

EXERCISE 9

3. When will he start...   4. What will he do in two months?   5. Who went with his uncle...   6. Who(m) did he go with...   7. Who found a nice apartment?
8. What did they find near the university?   9. Who needs a roommate?   10. What does Glenn need?
11. Who called several friends?   12. Who(m) did Glenn call?   13. Who else needs a roommate?   14. What does Sean need?   15. Who will share his apartment with Sean?   16. Who(m) will Glenn share his apartment with?

EXERCISE 10

Oral practice; intonation.

EXERCISE 11

Jim: I am   Catherine: isn't she?   Jim: she is.
Catherine: don't you?   Jim: we do.
Catherine: won't you?   Jim: I will/we will.
Catherine: aren't you?   Jim: I am.
Guillermo: do you?   Chris: I don't.; are you?
Chris: did you?   Guillermo: isn't it?
Chris: it is.   Guillermo: shouldn't it?

EXERCISE 12

Oral practice; intonation.

Unit 5

Modals of Probability and Possibility

1. is   2. must be   3. must work   4. could be
5. must use   6. could be; might be (or vice-versa)
7. may; could (or vice-versa)   8. doesn't have; could
have   9. must not/must   10. could; might (or vice-versa)

1. She must like chocolate.   2. She might be a nurse.
3. He must ride a motorcycle.   4. They must be related.
5. Natalya couldn't be Oleg's mother.   6. They may not because Lin is sick.   7. He may not know that's rude.
8. She must be engaged.   9. She might not know how to drive.   10. She could be in the wrong class.

2. They must be drug dealers.   3., 4. They could/might/may have inherited the money, or they could/might/may have won the car in a contest.
5., 6. There must have been a dozen wine bottles. They must be alcoholics.   7., 8. Kathy and Tim could/might/may have had a party, or they could/might/may have invited friends over for dinner.
9. Kathy must have gone to one of those AA meetings.
10. She could/might/may have been at a store near the church.   11. Tim must have gotten drunk and hit him.
12. Gladys, the boy could/might/may have fallen off his bike.   13. Gladys, you must be crazy.   14. You could/may/might be right.

1. could/may/might be taking a nap./could/may/might be sleeping.
2. must not/couldn't be taking a nap./must not/couldn't be sleeping.
3. must be grocery shopping.
4. must not/couldn't be grocery shopping.
5. must be walking the dog.
6. must have been drinking coffee.
7. may/might/could have been playing chess.
8. may/might/could have been reading.
9. may/might/could have been roller-skating.
10. must have been smoking.

1. B   2. B   3. B   4. B   5. B   6. A   7. C   8. C   9. B   10. C

Unit 6

Past Progressive and Simple Past with Time Clauses *When, While,* and *As Soon As*

EXERCISE 1

Answers will vary slightly, according to students' interpretations of the pictures.

Case 1: 2. He was short and thin. He had curly/wavy hair and a mustache.   **3.** I ran after him./I followed him./I chased him.

Case 2: 4. I was on Rodeo Drive (and I was) shopping.   **5.** Yes, he was short and thin. He was wearing a hat, sunglasses, and a tie.   **6.** No, he didn't./No, he didn't have a mustache.   **7.** I shouted/yelled/screamed.

Case 3: 8. We were playing cards/bridge.   **9.** He was short and thin. He had a beard.   **10.** He was wearing a suit/tuxedo.   **11.** No, he didn't./Yes, he did.   **12.** We shouted/yelled/screamed/called the manager.

EXERCISE 2

Answers will vary slightly.
1. There was a man with a beard talking on the telephone./A man with a beard was...   **2.** A/The security guard was watering the plants./There was a security guard...   **3.** There was a line of customers/people waiting./A lot of people/Six people were waiting in line.
4. Two tellers were taking care of/waiting on customers./There were two tellers taking....   **5.** A lady/woman wearing slippers and carrying a little dog in her purse was standing in line./There was a lady/woman...   **6.** A young couple was holding hands and kissing (in the line)./There was a young couple...
7. A bald man with glasses and a mustache was reading the newspaper (in line)./There was a bald man...   **8.** A young woman was writing a check/signing something/filling out something./There was a young woman...   **9.** A young mother with a baby carriage was holding her baby./There was a young mother...   **10.** Just outside the door, a man was smoking./Just outside the door, there was...   **11.** Another man was outside washing/cleaning the windows./There was another man...

EXERCISE 3

Answers will vary slightly.
1. He was (sitting) at his desk (and he was) talking on the telephone.   **2.** Yes, he was. He was watering the plants.   **3.** Yes, there were. Another teller was talking to/taking care of/waiting on a customer./There was another teller.../A man/An employee was outside cleaning/washing the windows./There was a man/an employee outside...   **4.** Yes. (a lot of/six customers

were standing in line.)   **5.** It was a woman/lady. She was wearing slippers and carrying a little dog in her purse. She had long hair(she wore it up in a bun). She was wearing a short-sleeved polka-dot dress and a scarf.   **6.** It was a young mother. She had medium-length wavy/curly hair. She was pushing a baby carriage holding her baby. She was wearing a dress/skirt.   **7.** Yes, the man at the door was just standing there. He was smoking.   **8.** It was 10:30/ten-thirty/half past ten.   **9.** He was wearing a tank top/sleeveless shirt and bell bottoms/bell-bottomed pants. I think he was wearing a hat. Maybe it was a helmet.   **10.** I was talking to/taking care of/waiting on a customer.

EXERCISE 4

1. False — Veronica Rio ran after the thief when/as soon as he stole her jewels.   **2.** False — Ms. Rio was having a drink when the thief took her jewels./Ms. Rio ran after the thief as soon as/when he took her jewels.
4. False — While Eva Galor was shopping, the thief took her jewels.   **6.** False — As soon as/When the thief took her jewels, Eva said/shouted, "Stop, thief!"   **8.** False — As soon as/When the Gentleman Jewel Thief took their jewels, the ladies shouted/yelled/screamed/called the manager./When the Gentleman Jewel Thief took their jewels, the ladies were playing bridge.   **10.** False — When/While the Gentleman Jewel Thief was committing his crimes, he was polite/not rude to his victims.

EXERCISE 5

1. When/As soon as the thief stole her jewels, Veronica Rio ran after him.   **2.** When the thief took her jewels, Ms. Rio was having a drink./As soon as/When the thief took her jewels, Ms. Rio ran after him.   **3.** The Gentlemen Jewel Thief began to talk to Veronica while she was having a drink.   **4.** The thief took Eva Galor's jewels while she was shopping.   **5.** When the second robbery took place, the thief was wearing sunglasses, a hat, and a tie.   **6.** Eva shouted, "Stop, thief!" as soon as/when the thief took her jewels.   **7.** When the third crime took place, Mrs. Rox and her friends were playing bridge.
8. The ladies shouted/yelled/screamed/called the manager as soon as/when the Gentleman Jewel Thief took their jewels./The ladies were playing bridge when the Gentleman Jewel Thief took their jewels.   **9.** When the thief committed these crimes, he was probably wearing a disguise.   **10.** The Gentleman Jewel Thief was polite/not rude to his victims when/while he was committing his crimes.

TOEFL Exercises

Units 4-6

1.D	3. A	5. A	7. D	9. A	11. B	13. B	15. B	17. C	19. C
2. D	4. C	6. C	8. B	10. B	12. C	14. D	16. C	18. D	20. A

Unit 7

Similarities and Differences Comparatives, Superlatives, *As... As, Not As... As*

EXERCISE 1

2. more; than   3. more; than   4. most   5. neater;
than   6. more than   7. more; than   8. more; than
9. less; than   10. more; than   11. more than
12. most

EXERCISE 2

Answers will vary.

EXERCISE 3

1. the most; the least   2. longer than   3. thicker than
4. wider than   5. the biggest   6. the tightest
7. curlier than   8. more carefully than   9. less popular
than   10. more friends than

EXERCISE 4

1. T   2. F   3. F   4. T   5. F   6. T   7. T   8. T   9. F
10. F   11. F   12. T

EXERCISE 5

1. less; than   2. as; as; are   3. as many; does/takes
4. as; as   5. the most; the least   6. as; as   7. as many;
as   8. as; as; does   9. as; as; does/talks   10. more
than; does

EXERCISE 6

1. Mr. and Mrs. Callahan, Johnny is not doing as well...
2. Johnny doesn't seem...   3. Johnny doesn't concentrate...   4. Johnny's spelling isn't...   5. When learning
new lessons, Johnny isn't...   6. Johnny isn't quite as...
7. Johnny doesn't read...   8. Johnny isn't as...   9. In
music class, Johnny doesn't...   10. All in all, Johnny isn't...

Unit 8
Measure Words

EXERCISE 1

1. bunch   2. loaf   3. carton/dozen   4. head   5. jar
6. can/bag   7. box   8. bunch   9. bottle
10. carton/pint   11. pound   12. pound

EXERCISE 2

Sentences will vary.

EXERCISE 3

1. bananas C   2. bread NC   3. eggs C   4. lettuce
NC   5. mayonnaise NC   6. dog food NC   7. cereal
NC   8. radishes C   9. white wine NC   10. ice cream
NC   11. margarine NC   12. ground beef NC

EXERCISE 4

Avocado Ice Cream:
2 cups of milk
1/2 cup of granulated sugar
1/4 teaspoon of salt
2 eggs
1 cup of heavy cream
2 teaspoons of lemon extract

1 cup of mashed avocado

Cheese Enchiladas:
1 dozen corn tortillas
1 pint of enchilada sauce
1 tablespoon of chopped onion
1 pound of shredded cheddar cheese
8 ounces of sour cream

EXERCISE 5

1. There is no juice in the glass.   2. There is little juice...
3. There is a little juice...   4. There is some juice...
5.   6.   7. There is a lot of juice...   8. There is a great
deal of juice...

Sentences may vary.
1. All the children are in the swimming pool.
2. Most of the children are in the swimming pool.
3. A few children are diving into the pool.
4. There are a lot of children in the pool.
5. Several children are lying by the pool.
6. A lot of children are out of the pool.
7. There are few children in the pool.
8. There are a couple of children in the pool.
9. There are no children in the pool.

Unit 9
Degree Complements *Too, Enough,* and *Very*

1. too   2. not enough   3. not; enough.   4. too
5. enough   6. enough   7. enough.   8. enough.
9. enough.   10. enough.   11. too   12. too   13. too

EXERCISE 2

Answers will vary greatly.
At the caterer's:
No, ice cream isn't sophisticated enough and it has too many calories.
No, it's too rich and not unusual enough.
No, they're too heavy for dessert.

At the department store:
No, it's too tight.
No, it's too long and I couldn't move easily enough.
Definitely not, it's too sexy and has too many spots.
Yes, it's perfect. It's not too short, and it's loose enough to be comfortable.

Auditioning musicians:
No, they play too wildly and there's not enough space for their equipment.

No, they play too quietly and seriously.
No, they sing too loudly and they're not sophisticated enough.
Perfect. They play softly enough and the room isn't too small for four musicians.

EXERCISE 3

Mercedes: too many; too few; too much; too much; too little; too little; too many cars.
Robin: too much
Mercedes: enough; too few

EXERCISE 4

1. too   2. very   3. too   4. very
5. too   6. too   7. very   8. very
9. too   10. too

EXERCISE 5

Sentences will vary.

TOEFL Exercises
Units 7-9 Answer Key

1. C	4. C	7. A	10. C	13. A	16. C	19. C	22. D	25. D	28. C
2. D	5. B	8. C	11. D	14. B	17. D	20. B	23. C	26. C	29. B
3. D	6. B	9. D	12. B	15. D	18. B	21. D	24. A	27. D	30. C

Unit 10

Giving Advice and Expressing Opinions *Should, Ought To, Need To, Must, Had Better, Could* and *Might*

Sentences will vary.
2. You should explain that your heritage is important to you.   3. You should take her to a game with you.
4. You shouldn't do things just "to be like the other kids."

1. You should sit down with your husband and tell him what's on your mind.   2. If you both have jobs, he ought to do half of the housework.   3. You should take turns making dinner and washing the dishes.   4. You shouldn't pick up or wash his clothes if he drops them on the floor.

1. First of all, you shouldn't listen to your friends, but decide what's important to you.   2. You ought to talk to someone at your local community college about careers in nursing.   3. You should try to talk to a nurse about his or her work.   4. You should definitely change jobs if you're very dissatisfied.

EXERCISE 2

Sentences will vary.
1. He ought to look for a job with a band.   2. He shouldn't expect to become famous overnight.   3. He needs to pay the ticket immediately.   4. He should drive more carefully.   5. She ought to try to replace it.
6. She doesn't need to tell him she lost it..   7. She needs to get a really big key ring that easy to find.   8. She should always put keep her car keys in the same place.
9. He needs to call a plumber.   10. He shouldn't try to fix the pipes himself.

EXERCISE 3

1. must 2. should 3. must 4. should 5. should 6. should not 7. should 8. must 9. must 10. must not

EXERCISE 4

Answers may vary.
1. had better/should	2. had better
3. shouldn't	4. should/ought to
5. had better not	6. had better
7. should/ought to	8. should/ought to
9. ought to/should	10. had better not

Sentences with *should, ought to, had better,* or their negative forms will vary. Suggestions are:

1. Father to son: You should be more careful with your allowance. I can't give you more money every time you need some.   2. Student to teacher: Do you think I ought to major in chemistry?   3. Doctor to patient: You had better quit smoking if you want to live much longer.
4. Mechanic to car owner: You shouldn't drive this car on the freeway. It's too old to go that fast.

EXERCISE 5

Migalie: should; could Victoria: could Migalie: could
Victoria: could Migalie: should Victoria: should; might
Migalie: might Victoria: should Migalie: should

EXERCISE 6

Sentences will vary greatly.
1. He must bring a...to the Bureau of Motor Vehicles. *Explanation:* Identification is required. "Must" implies that it is absolutely necessary.   2. He might fail the...if he doesn't learn all the rules of the road. *Explanation:* It's a real possibility but not a certainty.   3. He shouldn't be nervous if he's studied enough for the test. *Explanation:* It's normal to be nervous before a test, but if he feels prepared for it, it will probably go well. A simple modal verb is used.   4. He ought to...before the test. *Explanation:* It's a good idea to practice parallel parking. This is simple, friendly advice.   5. Angelica must get... *Explanation:* This is required for registration.   6. She ought to... *Explanation:* It's a good idea to register early so she can get the classes she wants.   7. She should find... *Explanation:* It's not necessary, but it's a good idea.
8. She needs to buy... *Explanation:* This may be a matter of some urgency if the books are likely to sell out quickly. "Need" is slightly stronger than "should."   9. I must remember to buy her... *Explanation:* It's not obligatory and I am free to do what I choose, but I will feel terrible if I don't, so a strong modal is used.   10. I could bake... *Explanation:* It's a possibility or option.   11. I'd better remind my father about it. *Explanation:* My mother would be seriously hurt if he forgot about it, so it's very important that I remind him.   12. They ought to start... *Explanation:* It' always a good idea.   13. They mustn't turn... *Explanation:* They are required to turn it in on time or take a lower grade.   14. They must type... *Explanation:* It's obligatory. The teacher will not accept handwritten papers.   15. They need to go... *Explanation:* They can't do research without consulting reference materials. This is not just a good idea, but a necessity.   16. Diego ought to call... *Explanation:* It's a good idea, especially if

he's not sure what's wrong.   **17.** He should go... *Explanation:* It's a good idea.   **18.** He could take...if he has a headache or fever. *Explanation:* It's one possibility or option.

EXERCISE 7

Answers will vary.

EXERCISE 8

Discussions will vary.

EXERCISE 9

Sentences will vary.
1. ...should work outside of the home if they want to.
2. Men should wash clothes as often as women do.
3. Boys ought to learn...
4. Girls ought to learn how to...
5. Boys and girls should go...
6. Women should participate...
7. Women should become...
8. Teenagers shouldn't be able...
9. Students shouldn't study...

Unit 11

Modals of Necessity and Prohibition *Have To/Have Got To, Do Not Have To, Must/Must Not, Cannot*

EXERCISE 1

True sentences: **1, 2, 6, 8, 9,** and **11**

EXERCISE 2

2. you do   3. Does she have to   4. she doesn't
5. Do we have to   6. must   7. do we have to
8. mustn't/must not; have got to   9. Do we have to
10. mustn't/must not   11. have to; must; have to

EXERCISE 3

2. have to   3. 've/have got to   4. does Irene have to; has to   5. 've/have got to   6. 's/has got to
7. 's/has got to   8. have to   9. have to   10. have to/have got to

EXERCISE 4

2. You mustn't dive...   3. You mustn't go in...
4. You mustn't take...   5. You mustn't push.
6. You mustn't bring/have...   7. You mustn't break...   8. You mustn't have/bring pets/that dog here.   9. You mustn't eat or drink...
10. You mustn't hit...

EXERCISE 5

2. must not/mustn't/cannot   3. have to; must not/mustn't   4. doesn't have to   5. don't have to   6. have got to/have to   7. mustn't/must not/cannot   8. has to   9. doesn't have to   10. have to

EXERCISE 6

Answers will vary.

EXERCISE 7

Maria: didn't have to; have to/must; had to
Jose: did you have to
Maria: had to; had to; didn't have to
Jose: did you have to
Maria: had to
Jose: have to
Maria: must/have to; mustn't/must not
Jose: do I have to do
Maria: have to

EXERCISE 8

Answers will vary.

Unit 12
Expressing Likes and Dislikes

1. does too   2. don't either   3. doesn't either   4. do too   5. do too   6. doesn't either   7. do too
8. don't either   9. do too   10. doesn't either

EXERCISE 2

1. Ramon studies Spanish, and so does...   2. I don't understand Greek, and neither do my friends.   3. Ann doesn't like liver, and neither does...   4. Cheryl loves animals, and so do...   5. Elizabeth loves the English language, and so do...   6. Maria doesn't like to write in English, and neither does Dora.   7. Gennadiy listens to classical music, and so do I.   8. She doesn't listen to rock and roll, and neither do I.   9. I like the teacher's new haircut, and so do ...   10. Roberto doesn't like it, and neither does David.

EXERCISE 3

Errors are indicated in parentheses, corrections follow the word in italics.
1. ...and so (is) *does* Debbie.   2. ...and my brother does-n't (neither) *either*.   3. ...and neither (Fathi can) *can Fathi*.   4. ...and Alonzo (didn't) *did too*.   5. ...and (either) *neither* did Irene.   6. ...and Sato (isn't) *hasn't* either.   7. ...and you (was) *were too*.   8. ...and (nei-ther) *so* was Sheila.   9. ...and (either) *neither* will Ed.
10. ...and so (has) *does* Patty.

EXERCISE 4

2. G 3. C 4. E 5. D 6. J/B 7. K 8. A 9. F 10. H 11. I

EXERCISE 5

1. sort of / kind of   3. Brian: I did too./So did I. Daniel: I don't either./Neither do I.   4. Brian: I am too./So am I. Daniel: Sort of./Kind of.   5. Brian: I don't either/Neither do I.   6. Brian: So am I./I am too.
8. Brian: So am I!/I am too!   10.. Brian: Sort of./Kind of. Daniel: Kind of./Sort of.

EXERCISE 6

Answers will vary. The gerunds to be circled are:
LEFT-BRAIN: doing, sewing, working, writing, doing, meeting, buying, speaking, competing

RIGHT-BRAIN: swimming, skiing, bicycling, thinking, dancing, making, fishing. running, meeting, shopping, rearranging, decorating

The infinitives to be underlined are:
to plan, (to) arrange, to collect, to read, to relax, (to) do, to paint, (to) sketch, to sing
Gerunds to be circled: 21; Infinitives to be underlined: 9

EXERCISE 7

Answers will vary.
1. Gerund   2. Gerund and Gerund   3. Gerund or Infinitive   4. Gerund or Infinitive   5. Gerund
6. Gerund   7. Gerund or Infinitive   8. Gerund
9. Gerund   10. Gerund and Gerund

EXERCISE 8

Group activity.

TOEFL Exercises
Units 10-12 Answer Key

1. A	4. C	7. C	10. C	13. B	16. D	19. A	22. D	25. C	28. D
2. C	5. C	8. C	11. C	14. C	17. A	20. B	23. A	26. B	29. C
3. D	6. A	9. C	12. A	15. D	18. A	21. D	24. D	27. A	30. D

Unit 13
Present Perfect *Since* and *For*

EXERCISE 1

Past: 1. She wanted to be...when she was a child.
2. She moved...   **3.** She began...

Present: 1. She is studying...   **2.** She wants...   **3.** She is volunteering...

Began in the past and continues now: 2. She has studied...   **3.** She has wanted...

EXERCISE 2

Sentences will vary.

EXERCISE 3

Donor: haven't eaten   Interviewer: Have you given
Donor: have given   Interviewer: has it been
Donor: haven't donated   Interviewer: Have you had
Donor: haven't had   Interviewer: Have you been
Donor: haven't been   Interviewer: Have you traveled
Donor: have been; have lived

EXERCISE 4

Answers will vary.

EXERCISE 5

Count Dracula: since
Stoker: for two hours, since
Count Dracula: since; since
Stoker: since
Count Dracula: since
Stoker: since; for

EXERCISE 6

Sentences may vary slightly.
1. Dr. Moreau has worked at Mercy Hospital the longest.
2. Dr. Jekyll has worked at the hospital since 1978.
3. Dr. Zhivago and Nurse Nightengale have worked at the hospital for the same length of time.   **4.** Dr. Faust has worked at the hospital for _____ years.   **5.** Nurse Ratchet has worked at the hospital for over thirty years.
6. Dr. Doolittle has worked at the hospital since 1973.
7. Dr. Spock has worked at the hospital for over five years.   **8.** Nurse Candystripe has worked at the hospital for over twenty years.   **9.** Nurse Shark has worked at the hospital since 1984.   **10.** Dr. Livingston has worked at the hospital since 1969.

EXERCISE 7

1. Doctors have regulated...for some time.   **2.** Have you wanted to be a surgeon since...   **3.** Larry has been...since 1989.   **4.** My stomach hasn't hurt since...
5. Joe has delivered flowers to the hospital for two years.
6. Sylvia has known my doctor since they met...   **7.** It hasn't rained since 5:00.   **8.** The doctor has been with Doug for thirty minutes.   **9.** Medical technology has improved since the last century.   **10.** She hasn't taken any X-rays since 1995.

Unit 14

~~nt~~ Perfect and Simple Past *Ever* and *Never, Already* and *Yet*

(1) ~~~~ **(3)** told **(4)** has flown
(5) has met **(6)** has seen **(7)** went **(8)** saw
(9) has done **(10)** jumped **(11)** rode **(12)** hasn't
been **(13)** crashed **(14)** had **(15)** had
(16) fought **(17)** won **(18)** has been **(19)** have

EXERCISE 2

Answers will vary.
1. Have you ever found... **2.** Have you ever flown...
3. Have you ever fought... **4.** Have you ever broken...
5. Have you ever given... **6.** Have you ever met...
7. Have you ever had a... **8.** Have you ever worn...
9. Have you ever ridden... **10.** Have you ever seen...

EXERCISE 3

Answers will vary.

EXERCISE 4

1. Have you called/telephoned your travel agent yet?
2. Have you already bought your (air)plane ticket?
3. Have you ever lost a plane/an airplane ticket on a trip? **4.** Have you already made your hotel reservations? **5.** Have you packed your suitcase yet?
6. Have you found a pet/cat sitter yet? **7.** Have you already gotten your passport? **8.** Have you already applied for a visa? **9.** Have you changed your money yet? **10.** Have you read any travel books yet?
11. Have you ever missed a flight/plane? **12.** Have you ever taken someone else's suitcase/bag at the airport?

Unit 15

Present Perfect Progressive

EXERCISE 1

2. He has been sleeping. **3.** He has been dreaming.
4. He has been lifting boxes. **5.** She has been unpacking dishes. **6.** They have been moving furniture.
7. They have been moving into a new house. **8.** They have been sitting in the sun. **9.** They have been swimming. **10.** They have been looking for shells.

EXERCISE 2

Questions and answers will vary.
1. How long has he been sleeping?/He's been sleeping for a couple of hours. **2.** What has he been dreaming about?/He's been dreaming about his final exams.
3. Why has he been having a nightmare?/Because he's been studying all week. **4.** What have they been doing?/They've been moving into a new house.
5. How long have they been moving furniture./They've been moving furniture all day. **6.** Who has been lifting heavy boxes?/The man has been lifting heavy boxes.
7. What has the woman been doing?/She's been unpacking dishes. **8.** How long have they been sitting in the sun?/They've been sitting in the sun for three hours.
9. What have they been doing at the beach?/They've been swimming. **10.** What have they been looking for?/They've been looking for shells.

EXERCISE 3

Answers will vary. The pattern will follow "Have you been speaking only English/talking to your classmates?" and so on. The answers will include: "Yes, I've been speaking.../She's been speaking..." and so on.

EXERCISE 4

Sentences will vary.

EXERCISE 5

Jimmy: haven't been sleeping
Joel: Have you been feeling
Jimmy: haven't been feeling; have been bothering
Joel: Has something been happening; has been worrying
Jimmy: have been thinking; 've been studying
Joel: Have you been studying; asking
Jimmy: have been memorizing; have been trying
Joel: haven't been worrying

EXERCISE 6

(1) have been reading **(2)** have been reading **(3)** have just realized **(4)** has been **(5)** have been collecting **(6)** has been waking up **(7)** has had **(8)** has been **(9)** has been working **(10)** has been setting up

TOEFL Exercises

Units 13-15 Answer Key

1. C	**5.** C	**9.** C	**13.** B	**17.** D	**21.** D	**25.** B	**29.** A
2. D	**6.** A	**10.** A	**14.** C	**18.** D	**22.** A	**26.** C	**30.** D
3. A	**7.** B	**11.** D	**15.** B	**19.** D	**23.** D	**27.** B	**31.** C
4. B	**8.** D	**12.** B	**16.** C	**20.** B	**24.** B	**28.** A	**32.** A

Unit 16

Making Offers with *Would You Like*

EXERCISE 1

The pattern is "Would you like...a table, sugar or cream, them over easy, and so on.

EXERCISE 2

Sentences will vary.
First Date 2. Yes, thank you. I'd like that very much.
3. What kind of restaurant would you like to go to?
4. I prefer French or Italian restaurants.   **5.** What movie would you like to see?   **6.** Well, I'd really like to see

_____.

One Year Later 7. Want to stay home and watch the football game?   **8.** Well, I'd really rather go country-western dancing.   **9.** Want to order out for pizza?   **10.** No, I'd rather have Chinese food.   **11.** Well, do you want to go bowling and eat at the bowling alley instead?
12. Sure.

EXERCISE 3

Sentences will vary.
2. Want me to help you with your homework, son? Yeah, that would be great. *Explanation:* Both the offer and acceptance are quite informal because the speakers are father and son.   **3.** Would you like me to wash your windshield? Thanks. *Explanation:* The gas station atten-

dant is doing his job. The exchange might be fairly formal if the two people don't know each other.
4. Would you like me to help you with those packages? Yes, please. That's very kind of you. *Explanation:* This is a polite, formal exchange between strangers.   **5.** Would you like me to phone someone for you? No, thank you. He'll be here soon. *Explanation:* The man offering help is concerned for the older man and speaks to him respectfully.   **6.** Want some lemonade? Sure. Thanks. *Explanation:* This is a very informal exchange between friends.
7. This is a great city, Dad. Let me show you around. Well, that would be great, but I'm going to be tied up in this meeting all day. *Explanation:* This is a polite, fairly informal exchange between father and son.   **8.** Want an aspirin? Yes, please. *Explanation:* This an informal exchange between husband and wife.

EXERCISE 4

Sentences will vary.
1. Would you like me to call a doctor for you? No, thanks. I think I'll be OK.   **2.** Would you like me to show you around? Thanks, but I think I can manage.
3. Would you like some more coffee? No, thank you. We'd like the check, please.   **4.** Would you like me to see if we have your size in the back? Yes, please. That's very kind of you.   **5.** Do you want another hot dog? Sure. Thanks.   **6.** Would you like to see our video of the Greek islands? Yes, thanks. That would be great.

Unit 17

Requests and Permission *Can, Could, Will, Would, May*

Sentences will vary.
1. Would you tell me which bus goes to the beach, please?   2. Could you tell me how often it stops here?
3. Would you mind opening the door for me? I've got my hands full here.   4. Will you wake me up half an hour early, please?   5. Could you show us where our seats are, please?   6. Will you pick up some milk on your way home, please?   7. Can you lend me some eggs, please? I've run out and I'm making a cake.
8. Could you tell me where the immigration building is, please?   9. Would you mind handing me that box of cake mix on the top shelf, please?   10. Will you sing my favorite song , please?

EXERCISE 2

Answers may vary.
1. I'd like to, but I don't understand it myself.   2. I'm sorry, but I haven't got any money with me.   3. I'm afraid I can't help you. I'm scared of heights.   4. I'm sorry, but I've never changed a tire and I'm not very good with tools.   5. I'm afraid we're all out of orange juice.   6. I'd like to, but I've got to finish this report.   7. I'm afraid my car is in the garage, too.
8. I'd like to, but I have to be downtown in ten minutes.   9. I'm sorry, but I don't know how this copier works.

EXERCISE 3

Answers will vary.
1. Sure, I'd be glad to.   2. Yes, I will.   3. Of course, I'd be happy to.   4. Certainly, no problem.   5. Yes, I will.
6. I'd be happy to.   7. Sure, why not?   8. Yes, I will.
9. I'd be glad to.   10. Yeah, I guess so.

EXERCISE 4

Questions will vary.
1. May I spend the night at Suzy's?   2. Could you excuse me for a moment?   3. Do you mind if I smoke?
4. Would you mind if I brought a friend to class?
5. May I put one of these posters in your window, please?   6. Do you mind if I leave work early today?
7. May I open the window a little, please?   8. May I check this out?   9. Can I park here?   10. Could I visit the counselor, please?

EXERCISE 5

1. I'm sorry, but you can't sleep at Suzy's on a school night.   2. Certainly.   3. I'm sorry, but I'm allergic to cigarette smoke.   4. Certainly. I'd like to meet your friend.   5. Sure , go right ahead.   6. I'm sorry, but I need you to finish this project today.   7. Yeah, I guess so.   8. I'm afraid not. Magazines can only be read in the library.   9. Sorry, but there's no parking in this block.   10. Yes, you can.

Unit 18

Used to with *Still* and *Anymore*

EXERCISE 1

1. T 2. T 3. F 4. F 5. T 6. T 7. F 8. T 9. F 10. T

EXERCISE 2

Answers will vary, but all will include *used to/didn't use to* + verb.
Questions are:
1. Where did you use to live? 2. ... what did you use to play? 3. ...what did you use to do after school?
4. ...did your parents use to read to you? 5. ...did you use to have? 6. What did you use to look like?
7. Who used to be... 8. Did you use to live...
9. Where did you use to... 10. Did you use to wear glasses?

EXERCISE 3

(1) used to	(2) used to	(3) anymore
(4) used to	(5) anymore	(6) anymore
(7) anymore	(8) used to	(9) anymore
(10) used to	(11) anymore	(12) used to
(13) anymore	(14) used to	(15) anymore
(16) used to	(17) anymore	

EXERCISE 4

1. T 2. T 3. F 4. T 5. F. 6. F 7. F 8. T 9. T 10. F

EXERCISE 5

Greta: isn't anymore; still is
Holly: Does he still wear; Does he still play
Greta: doesn't play rock and roll anymore
Holly: Does she still look
Greta: doesn't have long brown hair anymore; is still; still has; still does; still does

EXERCISE 6

1. She always used to go dancing on weekends./She used to go dancing very often. 2. No, she didn't (used to have children). 3. Yes, she sometimes helps them/the kids with their homework. 4. She often used to travel. 5. No, she seldom/hardly ever used to cook and clean. 6. Yes, she often cooks and cleans now. 7. No, she doesn't. (She never goes dancing anymore.) 8. Yes, she does./Yes, she still goes to the beach. 9. No, she seldom/hardly ever goes out to eat (anymore). 10. She does the laundry every day.

TOEFL Exercises

Units 16-18 Answer Key

1. A	4. A	7. C	10. B	13. C	16. B	19. B
2. B	5. C	8. C	11. C	14. B	17. D	20. A
3. D	6. B	9. D	12. B	15. A	18. D	

Unit 19

Past Perfect *Before* and *After*

BEFORE ACCIDENT: 2. He had never seen so many doctors.   **3.** He had never felt so much pain.   **4.** He had played tennis.   **5.** He had sailed.   **6.** He had had a dog.   **7.** He had been engaged to Debbie.

AFTER ACCIDENT: 2. He had a lot of operations. **3.** He had to learn to get around in a wheelchair.   **4.** He needed a specially trained dog.   **5.** He got Connie.

NOW: 2. He's learning to play table tennis.   **3.** He sails. **4.** He competes in races.   **5.** He's engaged to Patty.

EXERCISE 2

1. How many times had you been in the hospital before the accident? Never./I had never been in the hospital. **2.** What sports had you played before the accident? I had played tennis and (I had) sailed.   **3.** Had you run in races? No, I hadn't.   **4.** Before Connie, had you had a dog? Yes, I had.   **5.** Had you been engaged to Patty? No, I hadn't./I'd been engaged to Debbie.

EXERCISE 3

2. He slept late because nobody had.../Because nobody had set the alarm, he...   **3.** Nobody had done the laundry, so Allen didn't have...   **4.** There wasn't any coffee because nobody had gone.../Because nobody had gone grocery shopping, there...   **5.** There wasn't any gas in the car because Allen had forgotten to.../Because Allen had forgotten to go to the gas station, there...   **6.** His boss had told him not to be late anymore, so he was... **7.** While he was driving, he looked in the mirror and saw that he hadn't combed...   **8.** He realized that he hadn't cashed his paycheck when he got.../When he got to the gas station, he realized that he hadn't...   **9.** As soon as he got to work, Allen found that he had.../Allen found that he had left his wallet at the gas station as soon as... **10.** When he noticed there were no cars in the parking lot, he realized that he had forgotten.../He realized that he had forgotten it was Saturday when he noticed there were...

EXERCISE 4

Number in bold before the verb is the correct choice.

2. He **1**/locked the doors, **2**/turned off the lights, and **3**/went upstairs.
3. When he **2**/got upstairs, he **3**/realized that he had **1**/forgotten to take out the garbage.
4. He **1**/went back downstairs and **2**/took out the garbage.
5. When he **1**/went upstairs to brush his teeth, he **2**/heard a noise.
6. By the time Mr. Wilson **2**/got to the door, the noise **1**/had stopped.
7. He **1**/went back upstairs and **2**/heard the noise again. It **3**/sounded like someone crying.
8. He **1**/went back downstairs, and again, before he **3**/reached the door, the noise had **2**/stopped.
9. By that time, Mr. Wilson had **1**/gone up and down the stairs so many times that he **2**/was dizzy. He **3**/went to bed.
10. The next morning when Mr. Wilson **2**/went outside to get the newspaper, he **3**/saw what had **1**/caused the noise the night before.
11. He **2**/was surprised to see that the cat **1**/had had kittens.

EXERCISE 5

2. He had walked the dog and let the cat out.   **3.** He was going upstairs to brush his teeth.   **4.** He went (back) downstairs (when he heard the noise).   **5.** To take out the garbage./He first went back downstairs to take out the garbage.   **6.** After he went upstairs./He heard the noise after he went upstairs.   **7.** He felt dizzy because he had gone up and down the stairs so many times.   **8.** He had walked up the stairs four times. **9.** The/His cat had./The/His cat had caused the noise.

EXERCISE 6

(2) went	**(3)** went	**(4)** had never worn
(5) (had) been	**(6)** has learned	**(7)** has also learned
(8) visited	**(9)** was	**(10)** had ever seen
(11) was	**(12)** was	**(13)** stayed
(14) fished/had fished		**(15)** grew
(16) fell	**(17)** got	**(18)** is
(19) is	**(20)** has	**(21)** has
(22) is teaching	**(23)** is learning	**(24)** isn't
(25) has written		

Unit 20

Articles *The, A/An, Some,* and Ø

EXERCISE 1

I/Indian; Prize; D/Indians

D/book; D/customs; D/ceremonies; D/Indians; I/girl; I/plantation; D/beans; D/plants

D/story; D/army; D/Indians; I/property; I/soldiers.

D/violence; I/peace; D/Indians.

EXERCISE 2

(1) a (2) the (3) the (4) the (5) a (6) the (7) the (8) the (9) a (10) the (11) the (12) the (13) the (14) the (15) the (16) the (17) a (18) the (19) The

EXERCISE 3

1. a 2. a 3. Ø 4. an 5. a 6. a 7. An 8. Ø 9. an 10. Ø 11. a 12. a 13. Ø 14. Ø 15. Ø 16. Ø

EXERCISE 4

1. B 2. A: Which milk? It's the milk that was in the refrigerator. B: Milk is a non-count noun. The problem is spilt milk. 3. A: Non-specific quantity. Trouble is a non-count noun. B: Some is not necessary. 4. A. Non-specific quantity. (It's a small lunch.) B. What's she doing? She's eating lunch. Mention of quantity not necessary.

EXERCISE 5

(1) a (2) some (3) the (4) the (5) a (6) The (7) the (8) an (9) an (10) the (11) the (12) The (13) some (14) some (15) the (16) the (17) the

EXERCISE 6

(1) the (2) Ø (3) Ø (4) Ø (5) the (6) The (7) Ø (8) The (9) the (10) Ø (11) Ø (12) Ø (13) Ø (14) Ø (15) Ø (16) Ø (17) Ø

EXERCISE 7

(1) the (2) the (3) the (4) the (5) the (6) A (7) the (8) An (9) a (10) a (11) the (12) the (13) the (14) The (15) the (16) the (17) The (18) Ø (19) an

Unit 21

Articles With Names of Places

EXERCISE 1

Words to be circled are in parentheses; names that take articles are underlined.

(Canada); (North America); the United States; the Arctic Ocean; the Atlantic Ocean; the Pacific Ocean; (Alaska); (Quebec); (Prince Edward Island); (Montreal); (Toronto); (Mount Logan); (Mount St. Elias); Rocky Mountains. The Great Lakes; Lake Huron; the St. Lawrence River; the Mackenzie River

EXERCISE 2

Individual writing practice.

EXERCISE 3

Answers will vary.

EXERCISE 4

(1) Ø (2) the (3) Ø (4) Ø (5) Ø (6) Ø (7) Ø (8) Ø (9) Ø (10) Ø (11) Ø (12) the (13) the (14) the

TOEFL Exercises

Units 19 - 21 Answer Key

1. D	**4.** B	**7.** A	**10.** C	**13.** A	**16.** A	**19.** A	**22.** C	**25.** D	**28.** A
2. A	**5.** D	**8.** D	**11.** B	**14.** B	**17.** D	**20.** D	**23.** C	**26.** A	**29.** B
3. B	**6.** D	**9.** B	**12.** B	**15.** C	**18.** A	**21.** D	**24.** A	**27.** A	**30.** A

Unit 22

The Passive

EXERCISE 1

3 Focus on subject: 1, 2, 3, 8, 9
3 Focus on result: 4, 5, 6, 7

EXERCISE 2

(1) was made   **(2)** was bought   **(3)** (was) moved
(4) were drawn up   **(5)** was limited   **(6)** was
designed   **(7)** was built   **(8)** was covered
(9) were cut   **(10)** were visited   **(11)** was named
(12) was called   **(13)** was nicknamed   **(14)** was
named   **(15)** was finished   **(16)** wasn't painted
(17) was/had been sent   **(18)** were moved
(19) were seen   **(20)** has been sold   **(21)** have been
notified   **(22)** had just been promoted   **(23)** are
both going to be employed/will both be employed
(24) will be allowed/are going to be allowed
(25) haven't been bothered/weren't bothered

EXERCISE 3

2. The boy's father, Donald Derby...   **3.** Derby had
run...   **4.** The boy was thrown...   **5.** Derby's daughter, Debbie, 3, was also in the car, but she was not....
6. The father was taken...   **7.** The driver of the bus...
8. He was taken to...   **9.** The Derbys were not...
10. Derby will be charged...

EXERCISE 4

2. The meals get cooked.   **3.** The dishes get done.
4. Parks are getting designed.   **5.** Historic buildings are
getting renovated.   **6.** Housing for poor people is getting built.   **7.** Classrooms got painted.   **8.** Trees got
planted.   **9.** The cafeteria got remodeled.   **10.** Salaries
will get cut./Salaries are going to get cut.   **11.** Employees will get laid off./Employees are going to get laid off.
12. New employees will not get hired./New employees
are not going to get hired.

EXERCISE 5

(1) got laid off   **(2)** got poisoned/was poisoned
(3) was served   **(4)** did not get delivered/were not
delivered   **(5)** got lost/had gotten lost   **(6)** got confused   **(7)** got torn/was torn   **(8)** was
interrupted/got interrupted   **(9)** got scared   **(10)** was
going to be held/was held   **(11)** got put/was put

EXERCISE 6

These are the phrases that should be crossed out.
Paragraph 1: by the turtles
Paragraph 2: by them; by the people; by the people
Paragraph 3: by them
Paragraph 4: by officials, by someone, by the government,
by them

Unit 23

Phrasal Verbs

Answers may vary.
(2) put on   (3) sat down   (4) put down
(5) cleans up   (6) picks up   (7) writes out
(8) turns out

EXERCISE 2

1. put off   2. look up   3. write up
4. put on   5. help out   6. look up
7. hand in   8. met up   9. find out
10. woke up   11. got out

EXERCISE 3

2. cleans up; takes out   3. turn down; music   4. turns off;
turns on   5. set up; put off   6. call off; meeting; set up

EXERCISE 4

2. ...cleans her room up and takes the trash out.
3. ...turn that music down!   4. ...turns the radio down and
turns the TV on.   5. ...set a meeting up...put the meeting
off...   6. call the meeting off...set another meeting up

EXERCISE 5

1. ...to cheer her up.   2. I called her up...   3. ...turned
it on...   4. ...take it back...   5. ...get by with it.   6. No
change possible.   7. ...went over it....   8. He showed
up at her house right on time.   9. He found it out.
10. ...came across it

EXERCISE 6

Answers will vary.
1. They forgot to turn them off.   2. ...turn off all the
electrical appliances before...   3. I called my family up
on Sunday.   4. I called them up.   5. He got off the
horse quickly.   6. He got off it quickly.   7. I took off
my wet...   8. I took my shoes off.   9. I looked it up in
the phone book.   10. I looked up the new address of
the movie theater in the phone book.   11. She ran into
her parents at the movies.   12. She ran into them at the
movies.

EXERCISE 7

Answers will vary.

Unit 24

Adjective Clauses

1. ...is a person that likes to talk about other people.
2. ...are young people who are between the ages of thirteen and nineteen.   3. ...are thieves who steal money from your pocket or purse.   4. ...are people that think they're better than everyone else.   5. ...is someone who doesn't drink alcohol.   6. ...is someone that thinks(s)he knows everything.   7. ...is a soldier that has the lowest rank in the army.   8. ...is an individual who spends a lot of time watching TV.   9. ...are people who are elderly.   10. ...is a guy that's a lazy good-for-nothing.

2. Dogs are pets that we call...   3. Piranhas are fish that people are.../...we see in hot...   4. The monkey is a wild animal that we see in the jungle...   5. The parrot is a colorful bird that we see in hot...   6. The polar bear is a big wild animal that we see living in ice.../...people are afraid of.   7. Cockroaches are insects which exterminators...   8. Dogs are domestic animals which scientists classify.../...we call carnivores...   9. Piranhas are fish which we call carnivores...   10. The monkey is a primate which scientists have...   11. The parrot is a multi-colored bird which we find inhabiting tropical...   12. The polar bear is a mammal which we find inhabiting the arctic...

Conversational definitions: shorter than the written definitions; vocabulary is easier

Written definitions: longer than the conversational definitions; vocabulary is more difficult/scientific

(1) experienced   (2) obsessed   (3) disciplined
(4) disappointed   (5) surprising   (6) covered
(7) shocked   (8) frustrated   (9) annoying
(10) exhausted   (11) worried   (12) relieved

Answers will vary, with the following -ed/-ing forms for each verb:
1. surprised   2. frustrating   3. confused
4. exciting   5. worried   6. frightening
7. fascinating   8. embarrassed   9. annoyed
10. relieved

Unit 25

Conditionals

1. were; wouldn't have   2. would live/would be living; didn't have   3. would have; lived/were living
4. knew; would work/would be working; wouldn't work/wouldn't be working   5. went; would learn; (It's understood that he doesn't go to school.)   6. would live/would be living; had   7. would be; didn't have
8. were; would bring/could bring   9. would be; brought/could bring   10. were; would have

EXERCISE 2

Answers will vary.

EXERCISE 3

Answers will vary.

EXERCISE 4

In all of these answers, the main clause can come first, followed by the *if* clause (comma deleted). The following contractions are used: *would've (would have)*, *hadn't (had not)*, and *wouldn't (would not)*.

1. If Mary hadn't met Gordon, she would've married...
2. If Gordon hadn't gone to medical school, he would've gone...   3. If Gordon hadn't become a doctor, he would've...   4. If Claudia hadn't had Mr. Stack for algebra, she wouldn't have...   5. If Mr. Stack hadn't been Claudia's teacher, she would've...   6. If Barb hadn't married Tom, she wouldn't have...   7. If Barb hadn't known how to speak French and Spanish, she wouldn't have gotten...   8. If Jan hadn't gotten pneumonia, she wouldn't have...   9. If Jan hadn't moved to Arizona, she wouldn't have...   10. If there had been birth control years ago, my grandmother wouldn't have had...

EXERCISE 5

In all of these answers, the main clause can come first, followed by the *if* clause (no comma). The same contractions as those in Exercise 4 are used in these answers, plus *'d (would & had)*.

1. If I had seen her, I would've given...   2. If I'd had some money, I would've gone...   3. If I had known you were in the hospital, I would've visited...   4. If we hadn't broken the law, we wouldn't have gotten...   5. If I had known we were going to be so late, I would've called...   6. If the cookies hadn't been there, I wouldn't

have eaten...   7. If you had been careful, you wouldn't have made...   8. If Lexi had been at the meeting, we would've been...   9. If I had had a car, I wouldn't have taken...   10. If you hadn't told me the news, I wouldn't have known.

EXERCISE 6

In all of these answers, the main clause (with the name, Eva) can come first, followed by the if clause (comma deleted).

1. If Eva moves to Tokyo, she'll...   2. If Eva learns Japanese, she'll...   3. If Eva marries Mack, she'll...
4. If she lives in Fremont, she won't...   5. If she doesn't leave Fremont, her life won't...   6. If Eva marries Travis, she'll...   7. If she lives in a mansion, she'll...
8. If she doesn't feel like herself, she'll...   9. If she marries Sato or Travis, her life will...   10. If she doesn't get married, she won't...

EXERCISE 7

Answers will vary. The possible verb forms/tenses are indicated.

1. *will/be going to/can/might/may* + verb   2. simple present tense   3. *will/be going to/can/might/may* + verb
4. simple present tense   5. *will/be going to/can/might/may* + verb   6. simple present tense   7. *will/be going to/can/might/may* + verb   8. *will/be going to/can/might/may* + verb   9. *will/be going to/can/might/may* + verb   10. simple present tense

EXERCISE 8

ACROSS:
1. lightning   9. FAA   10. uno   12. ow   14. shins
15. PR   16. mew   18. lei   19. Eden   21. sued
22. bad   23. hike   25. okay   27. INS   30. yet
31. N.C.   32. spill   33. RH   34. tie   36. horseshoe

DOWN:
2. if   3. gas   4. haha   5. nuns   6. INS   7. No
8. something   11. Friday the   13. wed   15. pee
17. weeks   18. lucky   20. cat   24. Inc.   26. aer
28. apes   29. ales   32. sir   34 & 35. to

EXERCISE 9

1, 3, 5, 6, and 10

1. make a reservation   2. don't eat your food in the restaurant   3. order another round   4. want more coffee   5. order an appetizer   6. like it cooked very little   7. ask for the check   8. ask for a doggy bag   9. the service is all right   10. ask for the manager

1. G 2. E 3. H 4. C 5. F 6. D 7. A 8. B

1. I felt a lump...   2. he might have died   3. I see anything...   4. I call...   5. I hadn't quit...   6. I might have...   7. I had the flu   8. you have...   9. the doctors hadn't...

TOEFL Exercises

Units 22-25 Answer Key

1. A	4. C	7. B	10. D	13. D	16. C	19. C	22. C	25. C	28. B
2. A	5. C	8. C	11. A	14. A	17. D	20. B	23. B	26. D	29. C
3. B	6. B	9. B	12. D	15. B	18. A	21. D	24. B	27. C	

GRAMMAR DIMENSIONS BOOK 2, TAPESCRIPTS

(Note: either the textbook or the tapescript should provide the vocabulary listed for these passages)

Unit 1 (Activity 3)

Speaker 1 (man): Tell me what happens on this holiday where you live.

Speaker 2 (man): Well, I live near New York City, and in midtown Manhattan, I think it's on Fifth Avenue, there is a huge parade on this day in New York, and you don't have to be Irish to celebrate in this parade. Most people wear green and they're in a very festive mood, and it's a huge deal in New York.

Speaker 1: Uh-huh. Any kind of special food eaten on this day?

Speaker 2: Yes. As a matter of fact, if you're Irish, especially, people like to eat—oh, what is it?—not sauerbraten, that's Germanó

Speaker 1: Corned beef and cabbage.

Speaker 2: Thank you, corned beef and cabbage. I don't usually do it myself, but if you go in restaurants or homes of Irish families, certainly for dinner or maybe even for lunch, you would have corned beef and cabbage.

Speaker 1: Sounds great. Now, for our next holiday, is there any special food eaten on this holiday?

Speaker 3 (woman): Oh, yeah. Food is the most important thing about this holiday.

Speaker 1: Is it?

Speaker 3: Oh, yeah. You eat a big turkey, you eat a lot of potatoes, yams, yams are always eaten, you eat a lot of vegetables, and you eat a big pie, usually pumpkin pie.

Speaker 1: Is this the holiday with cranberry sauce?

Speaker 3: Oh, that's right, cranberry sauce. I forgot about cranberry sauce. You have to eat that, too.

Speaker 1: Mmm, sounds great.

Speaker 3: Yeah, it's delicious.

Speaker 1: What about customs on a day like this?

Speaker 3: Um, customs. Well, it's really important that you get together with family and friends and people you care about and that you give thanks for everything that you have.

Speaker 1: Is this an official holiday? Do people get the day off from work and all of that?

Speaker 3: Oh, it's an important holiday. Yeah, usually you do get the day off from work and school, and it's a public holiday.

Speaker 1: That sounds warm and wonderful. A real family get-together. OK. Now, for this next holiday, is it true that the kids love it especially?

Speaker 4: (woman): It's a great time for kids. Kids dress up, parents make costumes, kids go trick-or-treating.

Speaker 1: Well, these costumes are kind of interesting, aren't they?

Speaker 4: Yes, kids are witches, kids dress up as princesses, princes, swordsmen, um, whatever you want to be.

Speaker 1: Oh, that's wonderful, that's terrific. This happens once a year?

Speaker 4: This happens once a year, right.

Speaker 1: Fascinating.

Speaker 4: Yeah.

Unit 2 (Activity 1)

Man: Every year around this time, middle of the summer season, people all over North America go to country fairs. This week, as part of our series on life in small-town America, Marcia Chandler is traveling around country fairs and telling us about the sights and sounds. Today she is in Petaluma, a small town in northern California. Marcia?

(background sound of fair/crowds)

Marcia: Petaluma holds its country fair every June, and every June farmers from all over the county bring their finest animals: cows, bulls, pigs, horses, even llamas, to compete in the show. But that's not all that happens here. Right now I'm standing by the fruit and produce hall. Oh, what a display! Magnificent piles of fruit and vegetables. The judges are looking at the tomatoes and are trying to decide which one to award First Prize to. Bill Andretti right here beside me is looking anxiously at his tomatoes. He brings vegetables to the show every year and usually wins several prizes, so he's hoping for another one today. Good luck, Mr. Andretti.

OK, let's move outside. Let's see what's going on. Oh, some musicians right over here are under the trees, and they're just starting to play. Oh, yes, there's quite a crowd. People are gathering around, clapping their hands, having fun. Ah, yes, and there are a few people who are dancing. That looks like so much fun.

OK, ah, what else? Over here to my left, oh, the baked goods! I'm getting hungry here. Cakes, cookies, oh, bread, freshly baked bread. Oooh, what's this? Someone's giving me a slice of cake. Oh, thank you. Mmm. Oh, chocolate cake, oh, mmm, this is wonderful, delicious. Mrs. Jill Anderson's secret recipe. Thank you, Mrs. Anderson.

OK, and over here right in front of me there are some—oh, wow, here's a cowboy, a real cowboy! He's riding past. (fade out) Oh, well, let's follow him and see where he's going. Oh, oh, he's going right over to this corral. There's going to be a western show. Let's follow.

Unit 3 (Activity 4)

Speaker 1 (man): Do you have any plans for the future?

Speaker 2 (man): Oh, sure, sure. I figure that after I graduate, first thing I'm going to do is I'm going to take a trip to Europe. I mean a really, really long one, you know, stay over—

Speaker 1: Any country in particular?

Speaker 2: Well, um, I do want to get to Prague eventually.

Speaker 1: Oh, in Czechoslovakia.

Speaker 2: Sure.

Speaker 1: Czech Republic I think it's called now.

Speaker 2: Yeah, I've always heard it's a really cool, fascinating place, but I mean, I'm going to go to Europe and stay a while, like six months or so. What I'm going to do is I'm going to get one of those, one of those rail tickets, it's a rail pass. You know what I mean. You can travel all over Europe with—

Speaker 1: The Eurail, right?

Speaker 2: Eurail, that's right.

Speaker 1: After your stay there in Prague, do you have any plans after that?

Speaker 2: Well, you know, I think while I'm in Prague, I hear it's such a great city that I want to stay a while. I'm going to try and get a job there for a while and bounce around Europe with my Eurail pass for a while. When I get back, I don't know, I don't really have any set plans, but I think I'll stay in Europe, and then when I get back, I think I'll try, ah, try the West Coast and pursue acting.

Speaker 1: Nice going, Thanks.

Now, my next student is a high school graduate and I'd like to ask her if she has any special plans following her graduation.

Speaker 3 (woman): Yes, I do. I have a lot of plans for my life, actually. But the first thing I'm going to do is I'm going to go to summer camp.

Speaker 1: You're going to go to summer camp?

Speaker 3: Mm-hmm, and just like relax and play and have a wonderful time because I will be going to college in the fall.

Speaker 1: So you're not going to study anything at summer camp or get some skills there? You're going to wait till college?

Speaker 3: Yup, I'm going to wait till when college starts in the fall.

Speaker 1: Very interesting. What are you going to do in terms of a career? Have you thought about that?

Speaker 3: Well, I think what I will probably do is study liberal arts for the first two years and then see where my interests lie because—

Speaker 1: You're feeling your way?

Speaker 3: Right, because I like a lot of different things, so—

Speaker 1: OK, thank you for sharing those very interesting thoughts about college, liberal arts, and your future.

Now, my next guest is a young fellow, and I'd like to ask him what his plans are for his education, college and a career.

Speaker 4 (boy): Well, in reality, I'll probably be a lawyer, which I want to be in the first place, but my dream is to be a baseball player, you know. That's what I want to be.

Speaker 1: Mm-hmm.

Speaker 4: I want to get married, have a couple of kids, maybe two—a girl and a boy. My wife, work if she wants, not work if she doesn't want because I want to make enough money to support the whole family. And that's what I basically want to do.

Speaker 1: Mm-hmm.

Speaker 4: I want my kids to decide their own life, and whatever they do I'm going to be supportive of. I don't care what it is just so long as they're happy. I'm going to do everything I can to make them happy.

Unit 4 (Activity 6)

Lisa: Hello?

(pause)

Lisa: Yes, this is she.

(pause)

Lisa: Oh, hi.

(pause)

Lisa: Yeah, I speak three, actually: Spanish, German and Italian.

(pause)

Lisa: Yes, that's right. I'm currently teaching English for international business here at Perry College.

(pause)

Lisa: Ah, from Asia, mostly. Most of them come from Japan and Taiwan.

(pause)

Lisa: Ah, well, they usually stay between three and six months.

(pause)

Lisa: Before this job? I taught English in a private language school in Italy, in Milan.

(pause)

Lisa: No, I didn't teach any business classes there. Mostly conversation classes and classes in American culture.

(pause)

Lisa: Um, that was from 1991 to 1993.

(with Gary's conversation)

Lisa: Hello?

Gary: Yes, hello. Is this Lisa Hartman?

Lisa: Yes, this is she.

Gary: Hi, Lisa, this is Gary Berman with Riga Language Academy calling about the job you applied for.

Lisa: Oh, hi.

Gary: Hi. Lisa, as you know, we'd like a little more information about your background and experience—questions we ask everybody. First of all, do you speak any foreign languages?

Lisa: Yeah, I speak three, actually: Spanish, German and Italian.

Gary: Oh, great. And right now you're teaching at Perry College, aren't you?

Lisa: Yes, that's right. I'm currently teaching English for international business here at Perry College.

Gary: Mm-hmm, interesting. Where do your students come from?

Lisa: Ah, from Asia, mostly. Most of them come from Japan and Taiwan.

Gary: Mm-hmm. And how long do they stay?

Lisa: Ah, well, they usually stay between three and six months.

Gary: And what did you do before this job?

Lisa: Before this job? I taught English in a private language school in Italy, in Milan.

Gary: Oh. So did you teach business English there, too?

Lisa: No, I didn't teach any business classes there. Mostly conversation classes and classes in American culture.

Gary: Mm-hmm. And when was this, when did you work there?

Lisa: Um, that was from 1991 to 1993.

Unit 5 (Activity 5)

Speaker 1 (woman): Well, this woman might be looking out her window. There might be blinds. And that might be her boyfriend pulling up and getting out of his car in the parking lot. It appears that it might be her boyfriend walking up a set of circular stairs, and I think it might be the boyfriend falling down the stairs on what looks like what could be a skateboard. And then I think the woman probably heard the noise and ran out her front door which was left ajar.

Speaker 2 (man): This might be a little girl looking out the window when she hears a car honking its horn. And that might be somebody coming up the stairs. It could be somebody reaching to assist himself coming up the stairs, and that might be a car pulling into a parking lot downstairs. And this could be a man walking up the stairs, and that might be the door opening to the apartment at the top of the stairs. And it's all about somebody coming home, it could be, and people waiting to see who it is.

Unit 6 (Activity 5)

Speaker 1 (woman): So what were you doing when you heard the news of President Kennedy's death?

Speaker 2 (woman): I was ironing my husband's pants, and I couldn't believe it. I thought it was a joke. It just devastated me. All I remember is that I was ironing pants. I think it was a Friday afternoon. I was a Cal graduate and living in Los Angeles at the time, and I sat down and cried. I couldn't believe I was crying. And then when my husband came, I mean, because I had three little kids, I went to church.

Speaker 1: What were you doing when you heard the news of President Kennedy's death?

Speaker 3 (woman): I was living in England. I was very young.

Speaker 1: Uh-huh.

Speaker 3: I remember it was the middle of the afternoon and I heard it on the radio, and I was standing by a fish tank with a tropical fish in it. And I remember I ran and told my father.

Speaker 1: These stories, they're just so moving to hear all the different stories. Do you remember what you were doing when you heard the news of President Kennedy's death?

Speaker 4 (man): Yes, I remember that day very well. I was working at an advertising agency in Phoenix, Arizona. And a sales rep came into the office and told me that Kennedy was dead. I remember thinking that it couldn't be true. I didn't believe him. And it was only after that, as we turned on the radio and got the news, that little by little we absorbed the truth, that he was actually, had actually been shot and was dead. It was a horrible afternoon.

Unit 7 (Activity 4)

Speaker 1 (woman): OK. So how many differences between a pizza and a hot dog did you find?
Speaker 2 (man): I didn't count them, but there are lots of differences.
Speaker 1: There's about 20, I think. Would that do?
Speaker 3 (woman): Uh-huh.
Speaker 2: Yeah.
Speaker 1: What are some of them?
Speaker 3: Well, first of all, a hot dog is longer.
Speaker 1: Uh-huh.
Speaker 3: Pizza's rounder.
Speaker 2: Right. And a pizza has more variety, you know, you have a lot of different toppings.
Speaker 3: Yeah, pizza has more bread, more toppings, it's healthier than hot dogs.
Speaker 2: I guess less fattening.
Speaker 3: Yeah, well, no, I think it's more fattening.
Speaker 2: More fattening?
Speaker 3: I think it is. But it's better for parties.
Speaker 2: Sure. A hot dog is great if you're at a ball game and you don't have much time.
Speaker 3: Yeah.
Speaker 2: And you can eat it standing up.
Speaker 3: Yeah, and you can eat a hot dog in fewer bites than you can eat a piece of pizza.
Speaker 2: And if you're going somewhere, you're walking along—
Speaker 3: Yeah, it's easier to eat.
Speaker 2: Going to a shop or job or something.
Speaker 3: Yeah, yeah.
Speaker 2: You can eat a hot dog easily.
Speaker 3: But you can't flip a hot dog.
Speaker 2: You can't flip it, no.
Speaker 1: No, no.
Speaker 2: Pizza is better to look at, more interesting to look at, I think, with all those different toppings.
Speaker 3: Yeah, you get more to choose from.
Speaker 1: Uh-huh.
Speaker 2: Vegetables and things.
Speaker 3: And it's cheesier.

Unit 8 (Activity 5)

Eliza: Hi, Jeff?
Jeff: Yeah.
Eliza: It's Eliza.
Jeff: Hi, how are you?
Eliza: Hi, I need your help desperately.
Jeff: What's the matter?
Eliza: Well, I'm cooking Thanksgiving dinner for the first time for my entire family, and I don't know how to make stuffing, and I know that you make a great stuffing.
Jeff: Oh, yeah. Let me—it's really easy.
Eliza: OK.
Jeff: First, in as little oil as possible, like a tablespoon, saute a pepper, an onion, and about a pound of diced mushrooms.
Eliza: OK
Jeff: Let them reduce. Throw in a tablespoon of tarragon and some ground black pepper.
Eliza: Uh-huh.
Jeff: Then when it cools throw it in a bowl with your cubed bread, the stuffing.
Eliza: Right.
Jeff: Um, then add one beaten egg.
Eliza: Mm-hmm.
Jeff: And a little bit of ground parmesan cheese.
Eliza: Oh, sounds delicious.
Jeff: It's really good, and it's fat-free except for the oil.
Eliza: Wow, great!
Jeff: Good luck!
Eliza: Thank you.
Jeff: Let me know.
Eliza: OK.
Jeff: OK.

Unit 9 (Activity 6)

Man: I think the whole thing, the whole over-population issue is really a myth. And I think the dangers are way greatly exaggerated.

Woman: I actually don't agree with you on this one because I really think that it's the most serious problem that we have to solve for the 21st century. I mean, I think that we really, we really have to do something about it. It's too important an issue to ignore.

Man: But people are too pessimistic. Take the media, they give just too much publicity to all this stuff about global warming and not enough resources. No wonder everybody, everybody is upset because they just believe everything they read in the papers and see on TV.

Woman: I know, but I think there really are too many people in urban areas, and I think if you look at pollution, I mean, look how many cars there are. I mean, the air that we breathe is just not healthy.

Man: Well, I feel that the world probably regenerates itself better than we think and the world is very big and its resources are great and very powerful.

Woman: Right, I do agree with you. I do think that the world's resources are great. But I just think that we need to take better care of them.

Man: OK.

Unit 10 (Activity 7)

Man: So you think that smoking should be banned in all public places?

Woman: Yes, that's right, all public places. That means restaurants, places of business, public bathrooms. I just feel that people need to feel that they can enjoy a meal in surroundings where people are not likely to smoke.

Man: You think that restaurants ought to be smoke-free?

Woman: That's right, restaurants definitely should be smoke-free.

Man: And people need to feel that they can have an enjoyable meal where there's no smoking?

Woman: That's exactly what I feel. And I also feel that drug stores and restaurants shouldn't sell cigarettes and that there should be special stores where cigarettes are sold and that way they can be strictly controlled.

Man: You mean like the government should set up a special group of stores, chain of stores, which are controlled by the government.

Woman: That's right, I think the government should do that.

Man: What about education, do we need to educate young people about the dangers of smoking?

Woman: Oh, absolutely we need to educate young people about the dangers of smoking, particularly I think it's the parents' responsibility, not the schools' and teachers'. They shouldn't do this. The parents should teach their children that smoking is dangerous.

Man: So you believe that the school and the teacher shouldn't do this, but the parents should?

Woman: That's what I believe. I think it starts in the home.

Man: What about advertising? Do you think that cigarette companies should be able to, you know, advertise or should not be able to advertise?

Woman: Oh, absolutely. I think it's very important that cigarette companies shouldn't sponsor any kind of sporting event. I think this is particularly bad for young people.

Man: So it's your opinion that there should be a law that cigarette companies should not be able to sponsor sporting events?

Woman: Yes, I think you could go that far. The government should get involved.

Man: Mm-hmm. What about medical research, should there be more medical research on the dangers of smoking?

Woman: Yes, once again, I think the government ought to spend more money on helping people to stop smoking, and that means they should do much more medical research and they need to research particularly I think the addiction and how people become addicted to smoking. I think banning smoking is not enough. I think we need to think about how to treat the problem.

Unit 11 (Activity 4)

Man: Oh, well, I don't know a lot about it, but I think one way is simply if you're born here in this country, your parents don't have to be from here. They don't have to have been born here. But if you are, then you automatically are a citizen.

Woman: Uh-huh.

Man: Another way is you have to get a green card, and I think after a certain amount of time having a green card, you have to take a test.

Woman: Mm-hmm.

Man: The test covers I think language skills and the American Constitution, perhaps history, and then I think you have to go to a special ceremony and probably do the Pledge of Allegiance.

Woman: Mm-hmm.

Man: Yeah, those are the only ways I know of.

Unit 12 (Activity 5)

Speaker 1 (man): Hey, what's your favorite sport? Baseball's mine.

Speaker 2 (woman): Um, soccer, I think.

Speaker 1: Hey, I like soccer, too.

Speaker 2: Yeah, it's fast, you know, it moves quickly.

Speaker 1: Yeah, it's becoming popular.

Speaker 2: Mm.

Speaker 3 (woman): Yeah. I also like to watch basketball.

Speaker 2: Same reason, right?

Speaker 1: So do I.

Speaker 3: Because it's so quick.

Speaker 2: Yeah.

Speaker 1: Action all the time.

Speaker 2: So what do you like to play, like if you're going to play?

Speaker 1: Well, actually I play a little tennis, but I like to watch baseball.

Speaker 2: Do you like to watch it live or on television—which do you prefer?

Speaker 1: I think baseball on television because unless you have a great seat at the ball park, it's hard to see it.

Speaker 2: Oh, really? I like to watch it live.

Speaker 3: So do I.

Speaker 2: Yeah.

Speaker 3: Absolutely. Much better. It's more exciting. Plus you get to eat, really eat.

Speaker 2: Well, I guess you could eat at home, too.

Speaker 3: That's true, but I don't want to cook. So do you get to play a lot of sports?

Speaker 1: Well, I played a lot at school. I played some baseball, I played some soccer, and I don't have much time, you know, getting together with a team is hard so I play a little tennis, just two people.

Speaker 2: Did you ever play volleyball?

Speaker 3: I did as a kid, but no, not anymore, yeah.

Unit 13 (Activity 4)

Interviewer: How long have you worked as a word processor?

Patrick: I've been at Smithton and Banks' firm for seven years now. Wow, it's hard to believe since 1990. And during that time in my role as office manager, office manager is really not an appropriate role, I've done a lot more than just manage the office. I've overhauled the whole systems management, I've reorganized the EDS, electronic document storage system, and I've also implemented new, more efficient software.

Interviewer: OK. What software have you implemented?

Patrick: They were using something else, and I've switched us over to Microsoft Word.

Interviewer: What were you using previously?

Patrick: Syntrex, which was getting pretty dated.

Interviewer: Mm-hmm.

Unit 14 (Activity 8)

Speaker 1 (woman): So it sounds like you've traveled a lot. Where, France—

Speaker 2 (man): I've traveled mostly in Europe, western Europe.

Speaker 1: Wow!

Speaker 2: France, Italy, Spain. And where have you traveled?

Speaker 1: I've traveled a lot in Italy and a little bit in France and a lot of, you know, backpacking and that kind of thing. That's how I traveled.

Speaker 2: When? In the summer, fall, winter—

Speaker 1: Well, mostly in the spring and summer when I was in my 20s, you know, late 20s.

Speaker 2: And as far as transportation, did you ever use a train or plane or was it always on foot?

Speaker 1: No, I'd fly over there. I certainly couldn't walk.

Speaker 2: You couldn't swim the Atlantic, no.

Speaker 1: But I, yeah, mostly backpacking but, you know, I'd take the train, sure. You, what did you do? How did you travel?

Speaker 2: Well, I'm a lazy guy, and I drove when I was out in the countryside, and of course I flew over to Europe, but then I would taxi in the big cities and get a car and drive where I wanted to go.

Speaker 1: How much time did you spend in these countries?

Speaker 2: I would try to get at least three weeks so I didn't feel rushed.

Speaker 1: Oh, that's great.

Speaker 2: I like to do it sort of on the spur of the moment. Did you stay in hostels—

Speaker 1: Yeah, and sometime just, you know, under the stars. And you?

Speaker 2: So in good weather you'd actually camp out and sleep out in some farmer's field?

Speaker 1: Yeah. That's right, in a barn somewhere, we'd knock on the door and ask if that was OK. You know, in Europe they're pretty hospitable—

Speaker 2: Yeah, they understand that, that they're welcoming to the backpacker and—

Speaker 1: Yeah, they're pretty used to us. And you, where did you stay? Did you ever—I guess you never backpacked?

Speaker 2: Oh, no, no, no, no. I love my comfort.

Speaker 1: So have you ever stayed in a hostel or inexpensive hotel?

Speaker 2: No, I never have.

Speaker 1: Wow.

Unit 15 (Activity 4)

Man: It is so good to see you. I can't believe we haven't run into each other before.

Woman: I know. How long have you lived here?

Man: Six years.

Woman: My God.

Man: Yeah, since 1991 I've lived here.

Woman: I've been here for about five years.

Man: That's amazing. And you work just around the block?

Woman: Yes, I do.

Man: Wow. What have you been doing?

Woman: Well, I work as an editor.

Man: Uh-huh.

Woman: That's really been going really well.

Man: Good.

Woman: Lots of long hours. I've also been on—I took sailing lessons.

Man: Oh, terrific. Are you still mountain climbing, too?

Woman: I am, I do mountain climb.

Man: That's great, oh, that's terrific. How's Eddy?

Woman: Eddy is great. Eddy is really terrific.

Man: Good. What's he up to?

Woman: He is working in a law firm, he works really, really long hours, and we have a daughter.

Man: Oh, congratulations! I had no idea.

Woman: Thank you.

Woman: Her name is Sarah, she's five, and she's beautiful.

Man: How old is she now?

Man: Oh, gosh, I haven't seen you for so long.

Woman: I know. What are you doing?

Man: Well, I have two children.

Woman: You do? Oh, that's great!

Man: I've been busy being a dad, yes, you know, when I'm not doing the dry cleaning thing.

Woman: So, are you still doing the dry cleaning thing?

Man: Yeah, we're up to four stores now. We just opened one in Somerville.

Woman: Is your wife working with you?

Man: Yeah, yeah, when she can, you know, when she's not with the kids.

Woman: Oh, I know—

Man: Yeah, Michael and Katie. Michael's four and Katie's about to turn one.

Woman: Oh, that's great. Well, I'm literally running to a PTA meeting, so—

Man: Great to see you. I know where you work now, so I'll call you.

Woman: OK, great.

Man: Good to see you. Bye.

Woman: Bye.

Unit 16 (Activity 3)

Woman: Hi.

Man: Hi, thanks for coming early and helping me set up.

Woman: No problem.

Man: I really want this to be a good party.

Woman: Oh, it will be.

Man: Well, I'm kind of nervous about it. Can I ask your advice?

Woman: Sure.

Man: What do I do if I run out of food and somebody asks me for more because I don't know if I have enough and how much people are going to eat? What do I say if somebody asks me for something and I don't have it?

Woman: Oh, look, don't worry about it. You can simply say, "Would you care for some pizza? It's right around the corner, we can order some, but I did run out of salad." Or you could say, "Would you like some Chinese? There's a Chinese place around the corner." It's no big deal.

Man: I never thought of that. Having stuff delivered. OK.

Woman: Sure.

Man: What happens if somebody starts smoking? I didn't put out any ashtrays because I don't let people smoke in my house, but what do I say to them if somebody does?

Woman: Well, you simply say, Look, would you mind smoking outside? This is a non-smoking house."

Man: That's not rude?

Woman: No, of course not. It's your home. You know, if they won't comply, well, then just throw them out. I mean, you know, what are you going to do? I mean, it's your home, seriously, you know, people are very willing to compromise, you know. And actually you might not even have that problem because if people don't see ashtrays—

Man: Maybe I won't have to say anything.

Woman: Exactly, exactly. Anything else?

Man: Yeah.

Woman: You know what I have a problem with sometimes? Getting people to get up to dance.

Man: Me, too.

Woman: They just sit there, they're like against the wall—You know, I would, and I've done it before, I said, How would you people like to do a group activity, like the Macarena or something like that?"

Man: The hokey-pokey.

Woman: The hokey-pokey, of course, right, exactly, yeah.

Man: Yeah, I never thought of that, ask to do a group dance.

Woman: Yeah, yeah, sure.

Man: Good thinking.

Woman: Yeah, it usually works. It loosens people up.

Man: Yeah.

Unit 17 (Activity 6)

Man: Question No. 1: Agnes, you are in the book store with a friend standing in line to buy a text book that you need for class later that day. You realize that you left your wallet at home and you want your friend to lend you $20 to pay for he book. What do you do?

Agnes: Oh, I would say, Oh, my God, I left my wallet at home. Please give me some money."

Man: Eliza, same question.

Eliza: I would say, "I left my wallet at home. Would you be able to lend me some money?"

Man: Great. Question No. 2: Agnes, you've just heard about a new teaching assistanceship in your field and you feel that you're qualified. You need to ask your teacher for a letter of recommendation. How do you do that?

Agnes: I would say, "I heard there's a teaching assistantship in the next district and I really would like this job. I'm qualified. Could you please write me a letter of rec-

ommendation? I need one."

Man: Good. Eliza, same question.

Eliza: I think I would do the same thing. I'd explain how much I wanted the teaching assistanceship, and I would ask him or her if they would be so kind as to write me a recommendation.

Man: Good. Question No. 3 Eliza, you are visiting a close friend's elderly mother. She has made a peach pie, and you'd love to have a second piece. Your friend has told you that her mother loves to feed people, so you know it wouldn't be rude to ask for another piece. What do you do?

Eliza: I would say, "This is the best peach pie I have ever eaten. Could I have a second piece?"

Man: Flatter her into a second piece. Larry, same question.

Larry: Oh, I love peach pie, and knowing she loves to feed people, I wouldn't hesitate to ask for a second piece.

Unit 18 (Activity 5)

Speaker 1 (man): Since you have decades more experience in the world than I have, can you tell me in your lifetime what changes have you seen?

Speaker 2 (man): Well, I think the computer has changed things more since I was a young man than anything else. It's amazing how fast you can get information. You go to the doctor's office and they press a couple of buttons and they find out when you were last there and what medication you're on and stuff like that.

Speaker 3 (woman): When I first got married, using the telephone was too expensive. I used to write my family.

Speaker 1: Really?

Speaker 3: Yes, of course. Absolutely.

Speaker 1: Do you know people don't write letters anymore?

Speaker 3: I know, but I believe that it's probably sent by, you know, what is that called?

Speaker 1: Electronic?

Speaker 3: Yes, electronic mail.

Speaker 1: Well, it's the computer again.

Speaker 3: Yes, yes.

Speaker 1: What other changes?

Speaker 2: Well, I think things have sped up kind of generally, like isn't there an airplane that can fly you from New York City to London in like three hours?

Speaker 3: Oh, yes.

Speaker 1: That's the Concorde.

Speaker 2: The Concorde, that's it.

Speaker 3: And even everyday things, you know, like going shopping. I didn't go shopping in big supermarkets. I went from store to store. I went to the butcher and the produce man and the butter and egg man.

Speaker 2: And there's less use of cash these days, you know, you give them a credit card and push through a slot—

Speaker 3: Absolutely.

Speaker 2: And they know what your account balance is.

Speaker 3: Right. And I had a running bill at my grocer's. Really, I mean—

Speaker 1: You mean you bought groceries on credit?

Speaker 3: Oh, absolutely. He knew everyone in the neighborhood.

Speaker 1: Really. Thank you.

Unit 19 (Activity 5)

Man: So Harriet, tell me, when did you get married?

Harriet: Oh, I got married in 1955.

Man: Had you been living on your own up till then?

Harriet: No. You know, in those days, we jut didn't do that. No, I lived at home with my mother. And I still had a sister at home. No, I married my husband, I went from my mother's house to my husband's home. It literally was my husband's home. My in-laws had a two-family home, and they fixed the first floor up very nice for us.

Man: So after you got married, you stayed in the town where you grew up?

Harriet: I think it was two towns over, but yes, for all intents and purposes, it was very close.

Man: Mm-hmm.

Harriet: So I lived in the next town. It wasn't very far from my mother at all. And I lived with my in-laws which turned out to be very good because I had two children, one and a half years apart, and I had my in-laws in the same house to help me with them, and my mother and my sister were in the next town.

Man: Oh, it sounds terrific. By the time you had the children, were you still working at a job as well?

Harriet: Oh, no, I had quit my job in order to marry my husband. He worked nights.

Man: Well, had your daughter been born before your husband got his new job at the advertising agency?

Harriet: Oh yes, I believe—let me see. She had been born, I think she actually had been born a week after my husband got the job at the ad agency, yes. Yes, because we were very, very happy—

Unit 20 (Activity 6)

Man: So what was one of your favorite toys growing up?

Woman: I had a Barbie doll.

Man: Oh.

Woman: I loved playing with my Barbie doll. I mean, I would say that was like one of the hardest things to like give up when I knew it was time to like stop playing with my dolls.

Man: Mm-hmm.

Woman: I would like make up stories with her, and of course there was Ken and, you know, it leads to problems later in life. But I loved playing with my dolls. It was great. Did you have a favorite toy?

Man: Believe it or not, I kind of liked playing with dolls, too. My older sister had Barbie and she had Ken and she had the Barbie fashion show stage.

Woman: Oh, I had that.

Man: Yeah?

Woman: Uh-huh.

Man: And she'd be Barbie and I'd be Ken and kick her off the stage and, you know, and not let Barbie back on. But I had another doll, too, a ventriloquist doll, you know, where you don't move your lipsó

Woman: Right, right.

Man: Yeah, and he had this string on the back of his head so his mouth would move.

Woman: Did you have like boy toys?

Man: Um, I wasn't really into GI Joe and the soldiers, but I had a very impressive toy gun collection. Yeah, I had a bazooka and another one that was seven guns in one. Oh, it was amazing.

Woman: Wow, that's enough for me!

Man: It was too much for me.

Unit 21 (Activity 5)

Man: Irma, I have vacation time coming up. I'm thinking about going someplace in Latin America. Where should I go?

Irma: Oh, you're asking me? Go to Mexico City.

Man: Really. To Mexico City?

Irma: Of course. I spent all my childhood there, and I was very happy. But I think the best part of Mexico City is that it's the most crowded city in the world. I don't know if you're—

Man: It's the most crowded?

Irma: Yes. I'm not trying to scare you, really.

Man: Is it more crowded than Tokyo?

Irma: It is. Well, not in that sense, because Mexico City is bigger in extension, the territory, you know, is huge. Not talking about Tokyo in that sense. But I think that the variety within Mexico City, it's so big that you can deal at the same time with native Indians, with Spanish culture together, and also enjoy the benefits of, you know, of the occidental life, more Americanized world.

Man: Interesting.

Irma: Which I like, I love.

Man: Lots of cultures, lots of different peoples.

Irma: And eat in Japanese restaurants.

Man: Oh, good, Japanese restaurants. What should I be sure to see?

Irma: Well, in the first place, I think you should go to Coyoacan which is a little town that is built in between the city, and Coyoacan was built—it's a colonial town that within the centuries came up to be part of the main city, Mexico City, but it's not really integrated in terms of architecture, and it remains exactly the same with the churches, it has a lot of antiques and beautiful plazas and theater. Very cultural.

Man: So it's a small, ancient town within the city of Mexico City.

Irma: Exactly. That's correct.

Irma: Yes. I'm not trying to scare you, really. Um, well, you want to go to the Zocalo which is the main plaza for the national government. My father used to work there.

Man: Oh, I see.

Irma: Yeah, it's beautiful, beautiful architecture. I think it was one of the first cathedrals, if not the first cathedral, ever built in America by the Spaniards.

Man: When was it built, do you know, a rough idea?

Irma: It must have been 1521–1521. And it holds also—I started high school nearby, which was then High School No. 1, and it was the first university in the Americas, in America. You can't miss the university, which holds the best murals of the masters of Mexico.

Unit 22 (Activity 5)

Woman: So Larry, Paul told me you got ripped off a couple of weeks ago. What happened?

Larry: You won't believe this. I was actually in a bank making out a deposit slip, and I had a briefcase between my legs on the floor, and I was concentrating on what I was doing, right? And I felt something moving against my, my pants, and I wasn't terribly aware, and I looked down and my briefcase was gone.

Woman: Wow, that's terrible!

Larry: Which contained important papers, it contained my cell phone, and I looked aroundó

Woman: So that was all taken?

Larry: It was entirely taken. I looked around and the thief had left. I don't know whether this person was hiding somewhere in the bank or handed off the briefcase to somebody that left out on the street, but I was absolutely panic-stricken.

Woman: Sure.

Larry: And important things were taken. Andó

Woman: So what did you do?

Larry: Well, first I went to the bank guard who hadn't seen anything. Then I went to the bank manager, I filed a report, and then I had to go back to work.

Woman: Well, Larry, the reason I'm asking you about this is because my house was broken into last week.

Larry: I heard about that.

Woman: Oh, it wasó

Larry: What got taken?

Woman: Everything got taken. I mean, everything. We were gone maybe-

Larry: Nothing got left? I mean, all the valuables got taken?

Woman: Television, stereo, jewelry, money, you know, just everything was taken.

Larry: Was the back door broken into oró

Woman: No, I think they got in through a fire escape in the window, and we were only gone, I don't know, an hour and a half, and in that time they took everything.

Unit 23 (Activity 3)

Woman: So Jeff, what's your morning routine? What do you do from the moment you wake up?

Jeff: Um, I usually wake up around the same time every morning, around 5:30, and I turn on the radio and listen to the news for a bit and then I get up. And I usually put on an old pair of sweats and a tee shirt and sweatshirt and I go out and run.

Woman: Oh.

Jeff: I leave the house around 6:00, so I get back around 6:30 or so, and then I put on some real loud music. I turn it up really loud.

Woman: Oh.

Jeff: Well, I don't have any neighbors close by so it doesn't matter. Take off my running clothes and jump in the shower and sing along with the music.

Woman: Oh, that must be pretty.

Jeff: Like I said, there are no neighbors. And after my shower I get dressed and I go into the kitchen and make breakfast. I always make myself a pot of tea and then have a bowl of cereal and some fruit and when my tea is ready I sit down and I read the paper for ten minutes. And I put all the breakfast stuff away and I go and brush my teeth, make sure that I've turned off all the lights, and put on my coat and walk to the station.

Woman: Well, that's a pretty full morning. What about you, Agnes, what do you do?

Agnes: Well, I set my alarm for 7:00. I don't like it, but I do. And as soon as it goes off, I usually turn over and go right back to sleep for another 20 minutes or so.

Woman: That's just like me.

Agnes: Oh, really, I hate to actually get out of bed, and I put it off until the last minute. But I usually get up around 7:30, sometimes even later. So the first thing I do is go into the kitchen and make myself a cup of coffee, and then I turn on the TV. I watch the news or a breakfast show for a few minutes. And then I take a shower, very quick one, and then I get dressed, I put on my make-up, do my hair, and if I have time to grab something to eat, but usually I don't. (fade out) I'm just running around too much because I have to get to the bus stop and get on the bus at 8:15.

Unit 24 (Activity 4)

Lee: Oh, here's a good one. Pat, what would you say your ideal partner would be like?

Pat: Hmmm, oh, God. Well, let me see. My ideal partner would be someone who is amusing, definitely amusing. I mean, he has to be someone who would be funny. That's important for me. That's the most important thing. I mean, not that, you know, I don't want him to be ugly, butó

Lee: Right.

Pat: But he should be someone who has a sense of humor, who likes to laugh, who likes to be silly. Someone who's silly. What about you?

Lee: My ideal partner? Just like me. No, I'm kidding. No, I think someone who is pretty attractive, I mean, I have to admit it, it sounds shallow, but looks are important to me. And I think intelligence and a sense of humor and a real dedication to the relationship is important, but yeah, humor helps get through a relationship.

Pat: Oh, yeah.

Lee: Yeah, so that's my story and I'm sticking to it. What about you, Chris?

Chris: My ideal mate would have to be a person that is taller than I am, and when you're six-one that's not easy, and he'd have to be dark, I don't want a person who's blond or red-headed. I just don't find them attractive. And someone who makes me laugh. That's the most important.

Pat: That s the key.

Chris: Yeah, a commonality.

Unit 25 (Activity 7)

Speaker 1 (woman): If you had to choose three objects to represent American culture at the end of the 20th century, which ones would you choose?

Speaker 2 (man): Well, I think I'd choose a copy of the New York Times and a laptop computer, and I think an autographed major league baseball.

Speaker 1: Why would you choose the baseball?

Speaker 2: Well, baseball is the American national game, it's played everywhere.

Speaker 1: Right, right.

Speaker 2: And the baseball is the symbol, and I'd have some famous baseball players autograph it, sign it.

Speaker 1: Well, if you had to choose one, of all three, which one would you choose if you had to make a decision?

Speaker 2: Oh, I'd have to choose I think a copy of the New York Times, the most read paper, in terms of importance, in the country.

Speaker 1: Mm-hmm.

Speaker 2: Definitely include that.

Speaker 1: Good. What would you choose to represent American culture at the end of the 20th century if you had to choose three objects?

Speaker 3 (woman): I guess I'd choose a pair of jeansóLevi's, a Big Mac, and a copy of the TV Guide.

Speaker 1: And what do you think is like the most important if you had to choose?

Speaker 3: I guess the TV Guide would give the most information. So I guess if I could only put one object in the time capsule I would choose that.

Speaker 1: Yeah, that sounds good. I agree.